1970

This book may be kept

FOURTEEN DAYS

1970

Kirtl

Scott, Foresman and Company
Chicago, Atlanta, Dallas, Palo Alto, Fair Lawn, N.J.

33

Robert E. Knoll   University of Nebraska

STORM

over

THE

WASTE

LAND

L. C. #63–21894
Copyright © 1964 by Scott, Foresman and Company
Printed in the United States of America

CONTENTS

3 SOME LATER CRITICS *97*

". . . the theory and influence of Eliot . . . seem to me the most dangerous and nearly the least defensible of our time. They have grown upon our time with all the benumbing energy of a bad habit. . . ." Yvor Winters

INTRODUCTION

I

The Waste Land is both the most controversial and the most influential poem of the twentieth century. Every sizable anthology of modern verse includes it; and when smaller collections leave it out, the anthologists feel called upon to explain themselves. Critics and historians of modern literature invariably discuss its meaning and influence, and literary autobiographers give accounts of their first meeting with it. If *The Waste Land* is not Eliot's finest poem — about this there is also dispute — even Mr. Eliot recognizes it as his most famous: his inexpensive paperback collection is significantly called *The Waste Land and Other Poems*. What *The Rape of the Lock* was to the Augustans and *Tintern Abbey* to the Romantics, *The Waste Land* has become to the Moderns. It is inescapable.

The Waste Land is something like the modern epic. If an epic is "that rich vessel which contains the ideals and aspirations of the race," this poem is a mirror of a certain modern fatigue and dismay. For better or worse, it seems to define a twentieth-century sensibility. That modern men should see themselves as clerks carbuncular, victims of the considerable civilization which they have made, tells us perhaps almost more than we care to know about ourselves; but if we would know our time, we must know this poem. "For my generation T. S. Eliot's early poetry, more than the work of any other poet, has enabled us to know our world imaginatively," one writer has remarked. It has served two subsequent generations as it served Kathleen Raine.

But this ubiquitous poem did more than open the eyes of modern men to the world about them. It actually instructed them in what they could find in it. It did not so much free their imaginations from the sweetness of the Georgian world as it formed their judgments. The waste land of the twentieth century is in some degree Eliot's creation. Not all of us would think ourselves in rat's alley if Eliot had not taught us to, nor would everybody think this a time to shore up fragments against cultural ruin. Our lack of faith in what we can make of our world may have been shaped by what some call Eliot's defeatism. *The Waste Land* may even have encouraged political quietism, for it "describes an evil where no one and nothing is to blame . . . a disease which has so eaten into civilization that political remedies are about as useful as poulticing a cancer," R. G. Collingwood, the philosopher-historian, has written. One wonders to what degree Collingwood's identification of the contemporary disease, let alone his lack of prescription for its cure, has been determined by the poem that he praises. It seems to some thoughtful men that the central imaginative task of the new writer of the second half of Eliot's century is clear: he must discover an escape from the imaginative world of *The Waste Land*. This is no easy thing, this creation of a new world, for the pull of Eliot's poem is mighty.

The Waste Land has then an insistent claim on our attention. First, it is an esthetic monument of the first order. Even its detractors recognize its considerable poetic merit. In addition and as important, it is a cultural document, defining a modern mode of being. By attending to it, we can see ourselves in our historical place.

II

T. S. Eliot was singularly qualified to write a poem which was to become a "cultural document" of a society that thinks of itself as deracinated. Born September 26, 1888, in St. Louis, Missouri, of a college-founding family, the son of a mother who wrote poetry and a father who made bricks, he was sent "home" to New England for his education, first to the Milton Academy in Massachusetts and then to Harvard. Many years later, in 1928, he was to say that "I perceived that I myself had always been a New Englander in the South West, and a South Westerner in New England." At Harvard he studied philosophy, and upon graduation in 1909, he continued his education at the Sorbonne. After further graduate work back in Massachusetts—he wrote a doctoral dissertation on F. H. Bradley, the idealist philosopher—he again went abroad, to study in Germany and at Oxford. He has lived in England ever since and in 1927 became a British subject. That year he announced that he was now "an Anglo-Catholic in religion, a classicist in literature, a royalist in politics." Even so, a generation later in 1959 he told an interviewer: ". . . my poetry has obviously more in common with my distinguished contemporaries in America, than with anything written in my generation in England. That I'm sure of." Later he remarked that his poetry is "a combination of things. But in its sources, in its emotional springs, it comes from America." The British Order of Merit and the Swedish Nobel Prize for Literature came to him in 1948, and in 1963 he was surely the premiere man of letters in all the West.

The Waste Land is Eliot's second major poem, and his first extended poetic work. "The Love Song of J. Alfred Prufrock," which had occupied him since Harvard days, appeared in 1917. In October 1922 *The Waste Land* appeared in print, published in *The Criterion,* a London literary periodical which he himself edited. New York saw it the same year. It was an extraordinary and continuing success, especially with the young. Edmund Wilson was able to write in 1931 that "in ten years' time [Eliot] has left upon English poetry a mark more unmistakable than that of any other poet writing in English." For a brief moment others tried their hands at Eliot's fragmentary manner, but shortly his influence became more general, dictating subject and tone rather than detailed idiom. In his subsequent poetry, notably *Ash Wednesday* (1930) and *Four Quartets* (1944), Eliot has concerned himself with religious themes, as he has in a number of successful plays. His volume of critical essays, *The Sacred Wood* (1920), showed the way criticism was to take for two generations, and occasional critical essays have continued to appear from his hand. He has explained the relationship between his criticism and his poetry: "In one's prose reflexions one may be legitimately occupied with ideals, whereas in the writing of verse one can only deal with actuality." His observations about himself, like the writing to which they refer, have their ambiguities.

III

From the first, *The Waste Land* has been a battleground. Even before it appeared in print its mutations were violent; Hugh Kenner gives an authoritative account of its genesis. One can only wonder if ever before a major poem by a major poet underwent such violent editing as this one. Indeed, on the evidence Kenner presents, some may conclude that Ezra Pound made or remade *The Waste Land* so completely as to become Eliot's collaborator. Upon publication the poem met hostile reviewers. D. E. S. Maxwell gives an account of them and specifies several of the poem's critical issues which must be resolved by every reader. William Wasserstrom describes the use to which Eliot's supporters put the poem in America, and in doing so presents the American literary scene in the early 1920s.

That *The Waste Land* is understood as it is must be the result of explications provided by early critics. All such criticism begins with F. R. Leavis, without doubt the most influential practicing academic critic in Britain. The elaborate explication by Cleanth Brooks is the grandfather of all subsequent explications — and the best. All students of the poem use it. Brooks acknowledges his debt to Leavis and to F. O. Matthiessen, another early commentator and author of *The Achievement of T. S. Eliot*. Though Matthiessen explicates a bit, he examines the poem in its larger poetic and social context, being especially concerned with its system of allusions. Delmore Schwartz, in 1945 looking back a full generation, is able to assess Eliot's place in the international cultural scene. With him *The Waste Land* takes its place with the rest of Eliot's work. Assessments, explications, and generally favorable evaluations have continued to appear regularly. Most of them fill in the outlines laid down long ago by Leavis, Matthiessen, Brooks, and Schwartz.

But now, in the second generation after its appearance, critics have begun to scrutinize *The Waste Land* afresh. Following the lead suggested by Yvor Winters some years before, Graham Hough searches in it unsuccessfully for an underlying formal unity. While acknowledging its genius, he sees the poem as the inevitable consequence of imagism's faulty precepts. David Craig examines the poem's ideas and concludes that Leavis, Brooks, and the others have not successfully defended it against charges of defeatism. And Karl Shapiro, himself a practicing poet, finds the influence of *The Waste Land* and Eliot's work generally almost totally unfortunate. It has, he thinks, alienated most potential readers of verse. Like Delmore Schwartz, he views the poem in its widest context; but, unlike Schwartz, to him Eliot is no hero.

Altogether the storm over *The Waste Land* continues, now with increasing intensity. Perhaps it is natural for sons, even poetic sons, to rebel against their fathers and to ally themselves with their grandfathers. It may be that some members of this second generation after *The Waste Land* are reacting against Eliot as Eliot himself reacted against Swinburne. Be that as it may be, readers of poetry and students of the cultural scene may profitably observe this battle. Its outcome may determine the poetic imagination of the second half of this century. It is, as I say, of some importance.

Robert E. Knoll

part 1

THE GENESIS OF *THE WASTE LAND*

". . . it is doubtful whether any other acknowledged masterpiece has been so heavily marked, with the author's consent, by forces outside his control."

Hugh Kenner

"Since 'the form in which it appears in print' . . . remained for many years the most sensational aspect of The Waste Land, *this transaction requires looking into."*

Hugh Kenner

HOW THE POEM WAS CONSTRUCTED

This dust will not settle in our time.—Samuel Beckett

The Waste Land was drafted during a rest cure at Margate ("I can connect / Nothing with nothing") and Lausanne ("In this decayed hole among the mountains") during the autumn of 1921 by a convalescent preoccupied partly with the ruin of post-war Europe, partly with his own health and the conditions of his servitude to a bank in London, partly with a hardly exorable apprehension that two thousand years of European continuity had for the first time run dry. It had for epigraph a phrase from Conrad's *Heart of Darkness* ("The horror! The horror!"); embedded in the text were a glimpse, borrowed from Conrad's opening page, of the red sails of barges drifting in the Thames Estuary, and a contrasting reference to "the heart of light." "Nothing is easier," Conrad had written, ". . . than to evoke the great spirit of the past upon the lower reaches of the Thames."

In Paris that winter, Ezra Pound has recalled, *"The Waste* /145/ *Land* was placed before me as a series of poems. I advised him what to leave out." Eliot, from about the same distance of time, recalls showing Pound "a sprawling chaotic poem . . . which left his hands,

From *The Invisible Poet, T. S. Eliot* by Hugh Kenner (New York: Ivan Obolensky, Inc., 1959), Chapter III, "The Death of Europe," pp. 145-152. Reprinted by permission of the publisher.

reduced to about half its size, in the form in which it appears in print." Since "the form in which it appears in print," with its many sudden transitions and its implication, inhering in tone and cross-references and reinforced by notes, of a center of gravity nowhere explicitly located, remained for many years the most sensational aspect of *The Waste Land,* this transaction requires looking into. The manuscript with the Conrad epigraph and Pound's blue-pencilling has been lost sight of; John Quinn appears to have made a private bestowal of it before his collection was dispersed in 1924. From surviving clues—chiefly three letters that passed between Pound and Eliot in the winter of 1921-1922—one may hazard guesses concerning the nature of the original series.

The letters, though they were exchanged after the major operation on the poem had been performed, disclose Eliot still in the act of agonizing not only about residual verbal details but about the desirability of adding or suppressing whole sections. "There were long passages in different metres, with short lyrics sandwiched in between," he has since recalled. The long passages included "a rather poor pastiche of Pope," which was presumably the occasion of Pound's dictum, elsewhere recorded, that pastiche is only justified if it is better than the original; "another passage about a fashionable lady having breakfast in bed, and another long passage about a shipwreck, which was obviously inspired by the Ulysses episode in the *Inferno.*" This would have led up to the "death by water" of the "drowned Phoenician sailor"; Victor Berard's speculations concerning the possible origin of the *Odyssey* in Phoenician *periploi* /146/ had been in print for twenty years and had occupied the attention of James Joyce. The deletion of these passages was apparently accepted without protest. The lyrics, on the other hand, contained elements Eliot struggled to preserve. After they have been removed from the body of *The Waste Land* he proposes putting them at the end, and is again dissuaded: "The thing now runs from 'April . . .' to 'shantih' without a break. That is 19 pages, and let us say the longest poem in the English langwidge. Don't try to bust all records by prolonging it three pages further." One of the lyrics contained a "sweats with tears" passage which Eliot, after deletion from its original context, proposed working into the "nerves monologue: only place where it can go." Pound vetoed it again: "I dare say the sweats with tears will wait." It didn't wait long; we find it in a poem contributed pseudonymously to Wyndham Lewis' *Tyro* a little before the publication of *The Waste Land,* and later revised for publication in a triad of *Dream Songs,* all three of which may have descended from the *ur-Waste Land.** Pound also dissuaded Eliot from installing *Gerontion* as a prelude to the sequence, forebade him to delete "Phlebas the Phoenician," and nagged about the Conrad epigraph until a better one was discovered in Petronius.

These events are worth reconstructing because they clarify a number of things about the scope and intention of the poem. It was conceived as a somewhat loose medley, /147/ as the relief of more diffuse impulses than those to which its present compacted form corresponds. The separate preservation of the *Dream Songs* and the incorporation of some of their motifs, after much trial and error, into what is now *The Hollow Men,* testifies to Eliot's stubborn conviction that there was virtue in some of the omitted elements, whether or not their presence could be justified within the wholeness, not at first foreseen by the author, which the greater part of *The Waste Land* at length assumed. That wholeness, since it never did incorporate everything the author wanted it to, was to some extent a compromise, gotten by permuting with another's assistance materials he no longer had it in him to rethink; and finally, after Pound, by simply eliminating everything not of the first intensity, had revealed an unexpected corporate substantiality in what survived, Eliot's impulse was to "explain" the poem as "thoughts of a dry brain in a dry season" by prefixing *Gerontion.*

That is to say, the first quality of *The Waste Land* to catch a newcomer's attention, its self-sufficient juxtaposition without copulae of themes and passages in a dense mosaic, had at first a novelty which troubled even the author. It was a quality arrived at by Pound's cutting; it didn't trouble Pound, who had already begun work on *The Cantos.* But Eliot, preoccupied as always with the seventeenth-century drama and no doubt tacitly encouraged by the example of Browning, naturally conceived a long poem as somebody's spoken or unspoken monologue, its shifts of direction and transition from theme to theme psychologically justified by the workings of the speaker's brain. *Prufrock* and *Gerontion* elucidate not only a phase of civilization but a perceiving—for the purpose of the poem, a /148/ presiding—consciousness. For anyone who has undergone immersion in the delicate phenomenology of Francis Herbert Bradley, in fact, it is meaningless to conceive of a presenta-

---

*Two of them, *The wind sprang up* and *Eyes that last I saw in tears,* are preserved in the collected volume as *Minor Poems.* The third is now part iii of *The Hollow Men.* The poem in *The Tyro* is called *Song to the Opherian* and signed "Gus Krutzsch," a portmanteau-name of which Kurtz seems to be one of the components. There are many small signs that *The Hollow Men* grew from rejected pieces of *The Waste Land.* /147/

tion that cannot be resolved into an experienced content and a "finite center" which experiences. The perceiver is describable only as the zone of consciousness where that which he perceives can coexist; but the perceived, conversely, can't be accorded independent status; it is, precisely, all that can coexist in this particular zone of consciousness. In a loose sequence of poems these considerations need give no trouble; the pervading zone of consciousness is that of the author: as we intuit Herrick in *Hesperides,* or Herbert in *The Temple.* But a five-parted work of 434 lines entitled *The Waste Land,* with sudden wrenching juxtapositions, thematic links between section and section, fragments quoted from several languages with no one present to whose mind they can occur: this dense textural unity, as queer as *Le Sacre du Printemps,* must have seemed to Eliot a little factitious until he had gotten used to the poem in its final form; which, as everyone who has encountered it knows, must take some time. So we discover him endeavoring to square the artistic fact with his pervasive intuition of fitness by the note on Tiresias, which offers to supply the poem with a nameable point of view:

> Tiresias, although a mere spectator and not indeed a "character," is yet the most important personage in the poem, uniting all the rest. Just as the one-eyed merchant, seller of currants, melts into the Phoenician Sailor, and the latter is not wholly distinct from Ferdinand Prince of Naples, so all the women are one woman, and the two sexes meet in Tiresias. What Tiresias *sees,* in fact, is the substance of the poem. /149/

If we take this note as an afterthought, a token placation, say, of the ghost of Bradley, rather than as elucidative of the assumption under which the writing was originally done, our approach to *The Waste Land* will be facilitated. In fact we shall do well to discard the notes as much as possible; they have bedevilled discussion for decades.

The writing of the notes was a last complication in the fractious history of the poem's composition; it is doubtful whether any other acknowledged masterpiece has been so heavily marked, with the author's consent, by forces outside his control. The notes got added to *The Waste Land* as a consequence of the technological fact that books are printed in multiples of thirty-two pages.

The poem, which had appeared without any annotation whatever in *The Criterion* and in the *Dial* (October and November, 1922, respectively), was in book form too long for thirty-two pages of

decent-sized print and a good deal too short for sixty-four. So Eliot
(at length disinclined, fortunately, to insert *Gerontion* as a preface
or to append the cancelled lyrics) set to work to expand a few notes
in which he had identified the quotations, "with a view to spiking
the guns of critics of my earlier poems who had accused me of
plagiarism."* He dilated on the Tarot Pack, copied out nineteen
lines from Ovid and thirty-three words from Chapman's *Handbook
of Birds of Eastern North America*, recorded his evaluation of the
interior of the Church of St. Magnus Martyr, saluted the late Henry
Clarke Warren as one of the great pioneers of Buddhist studies in
the Occident, directed the reader's attention to /150/ a hallucination
recorded on one of the Antarctic expeditions ("I forget which, but
I think one of Shackleton's"), and eventually, with the aid of quotations from Froude, Bradley, and Hermann Hesse's *Blick ins
Chaos*, succeeded in padding the thing out to a suitable length. The
keying of these items to specific passages by the academic device
of numbering lines—hence Eliot's pleasantry, twenty-four years
later, about "bogus scholarship"—may be surmised to have been
done in haste: early in *What the Thunder Said* a line was missed in
the counting. "I have sometimes thought," Eliot has said, "of getting
rid of these notes; but now they can never be unstuck. They have
had almost greater popularity than the poem itself. . . . It was just,
no doubt, that I should pay my tribute to the work of Miss Jessie
Weston; but I regret having sent so many enquirers off on a wild
goose chase after Tarot cards and the Holy Grail." We have license
therefore to ignore them, and instead "endeavor to grasp what the
poetry is aiming to be . . . to grasp its entelechy."

That the entelechy is graspable without source-hunting, and
without even appeal to any but the most elementary knowledge of
one or two myths and a few Shakespearean tags, is a statement
requiring temerity to sustain in the face of all the scholarship that
has been expended during a third of a century on these 434 lines.
It inheres, however, in Dr. Leavis' admirably tactful account of the
poem in *New Bearings*, and in Pound's still earlier testimony. In
1924 Pound rebutted a piece of reviewer's acrimony with the flat
statement that the poem's obscurities were reducible to four
Sanskrit words, three of which are

so implied in the surrounding text that one can pass them
by . . . without losing the general tone or the main emo- /151/

---

*This incredibly illiterate literary society seems to have been wholly unaware of the methods
of Pope, or else to have supposed that a period allegedly devoted to "profuse strains of unpre-
meditated art" had rendered such methods obsolete. /150/

tion of the passage. They are so obviously the words of some ritual or other.

[One does need to be told that "shantih" means "peace."]

For the rest, I saw the poem in typescript, and I did not see the notes till 6 or 8 months afterward; and they have not increased my enjoyment of the poem one atom. The poem seems to me an emotional unit. . . .

I have not read Miss Weston's *Ritual to Romance,* and do not at present intend to. As to the citations, I do not think it matters a damn which is from Day, which from Milton, Middleton, Webster, or Augustine. I mean so far as the functioning of the poem is concerned. One's incult pleasure in reading *The Waste Land* would be the same if Webster had written "Women Before Woman" and Marvell the *Metamorphoses.*

His parting shot deserves preservation:

This demand for clarity in every particular of a work, whether essential or not, reminds me of the Pre-Raphaelite painter who was doing a twilight scene but rowed across the river in day time to see the shape of the leaves on the further bank, which he then drew in with full detail. /152/

"'. . . a piece of literary carpentry, scholarly joiner's work . . . .'"
[quoted from Louis Untermeyer]

". . . a poetic treatment of certain aspects of a civilisation, placing them in the perspective of time."

D. E. S. Maxwell

HOW THE POEM WAS RECEIVED

AND ITS CRITICAL ISSUES DEFINED

What must strike the reader most forcibly about *Poems 1920* and *The Waste Land* is their insistence on the setting. Temporal human affairs are presented directly within this setting, while their spiritual significance is left implicit, in the imagery and in the allusions to past literature. These poems present Eliot's vision of 'the turning world', a symbol first used in 'Coriolan' II. The characteristics of mechanical civilisation and urban squalor provide the necessary starting point for Eliot's investigation of the distress peculiar to the modern soul. The poetry is never concerned solely with the presentation of a picture of 'the turning world': the spiritual undertones are always present. But what most distinguishes the early from the later poetry is that in the former the streets, the houses, the music, the routine affairs of the people overlay the spiritual considerations and are essential to their communication.

In the final section of *The Waste Land* can be seen the first divergence from direct insistence on the surroundings. The method is still allusive — as it always is — but it operates now away from the contemporary setting. Composed, as will be shown, in the figure of Coriolanus, the Fisher King, and the lost father, is the notion of a

From *The Poetry of T. S. Eliot* by D. E. S. Maxwell (New York: Barnes & Noble, Inc., 1961), Chapter 5, "The Turning World," pp. 97-101. Published in England in 1952 by Routledge & Kegan Paul, Ltd., and reprinted by their permission.

focus towards which the instability and flux of material affairs should converge. From such convergence they will be endowed with a meaning which they must lack if there is no stable centre. This concept is symbolised — also in 'Coriolan' II — /97/ as 'the still centre'. From his vision of the world, which forms the foreground of this poetry, Eliot moves to contemplation of the true reality, contained in God, the still point. This process continues to the *Four Quartets,* where it is the social reality that is largely left implied, and direct contemplation of spiritual affairs occupies the foreground. But this is to anticipate.

Much of the poetry between *The Waste Land* and *Four Quartets* continues to stress the social reality. However, it is in *Poems 1920* and *The Waste Land* that we find the fullest account of the physical characteristics of 'the turning world'.

The Waste Land has been so many times analysed and dissected that some relief is found in a return to the refreshingly forthright comments made on the poem when it first appeared. The uniform characteristic of these is that none of them looked on it as a poem at all. It was considered, at best, as a series of slightly related separate poems. So assured was this attitude that *The Times Literary Supplement* was able to dismiss casually 'some references to vegetation ceremonies', not unimportant to the structure of the poem. The following comments on various aspects of the poem, as they are concerned with some of the fundamentals of the poetry, provide a useful starting point.

On the unity of the poem

New Statesman and Nation, 4th November, 1922, p. 140. 'Affable Hawk' notes that in the first issue of *Criterion* appear 'several separate poems entitled *The Waste Land.*'

Scrutinies, II. Alec Brown, in an essay entitled 'The Lyric Impulse in T. S. Eliot', decides that *'The Waste Land,* for all the suggestion made by calling it a poem, is but a set of shorter poems . . . tacked together.'

American Poetry since 1900 (Louis Untermeyer): '. . . it is doubtful whether *The Waste Land* is anything but a set of separate poems . . . a piece of literary carpentry, scholarly joiner's work; the flotsam and jetsam of desiccated culture . . . a pompous parade of erudition.'

On the system of allusion

Generally one notes the common antithesis indicated between

the true poet who looks directly on life and the pseudo-poet who looks on it through the spectacles of books. /98/

New Statesman and Nation, 3rd November, 1923, p. 117. Review of the poem by F. L. Lucas. As an introductory comment he notes that Alexandrian poetry finds 'in literature an inspiration that life gives no more', with the implication that this is to be deplored. The generalisation is unconvincing. Neither Pope nor Eliot ignores life, even the life of which literature is not a part.

Untermeyer, op. cit.: 'It is an anthology of assimilations — a poetry, as Mary C. Colum pointed out, 'of interest to critics and people professionally interested in literature; it appeals to their sophisticated consciousness, whereas great literature appeals either to our subconscious or superconscious minds — that is to something that either transcends our experience or is profoundly buried in our experience'. Eliot's poetry does neither; it appeals only to our acquired knowledge.' One may question the assumption that only our experience of literature is to be described as 'acquired knowledge', and that it cannot appeal to those parts of our minds open to other transcribed experiences.

Times Literary Supplement, 20th September, 1923: 'parodying without taste or skill' — adding that, 'of this the example from Goldsmith is not the most astonishing'.

New Statesman; F. L. Lucas: '. . . the parodies are cheap and the imitations inferior.

Untermeyer, op. cit.: Describes the allusions as 'weak burlesque'.

On the poet who might have been

On this issue we find Lucas and Brown united in considering Eliot a romanticist manqué, scattering occasional pearls among his litter. With this is coupled regret over the urban influence in Eliot's poetry, and nostalgia for a vanished rural impetus. Eliot, says Brown, is 'almost morbidly attracted' by the sordidness of city life. This critic looks in Eliot's work for passages he considers lyric, describes this as the outcome of Eliot's innate — and deliberately stifled — lyric impulse, and condemns the rest almost in its entirety. Lucas similarly: 'The first of the five sections opens in spring with one of the snatches of poetry that occur scattered about the poem.' Implied in this is refusal to look on the poem as a whole. He goes on to object to the 'young man carbuncular' as 'a typical instance of that squalor which seems perpetually to /99/ obsess Mr. Eliot with mixed fascination and repulsion . . . suburban sordidness'.

On the symbolism

Lucas's is the final word: Speaking of the necessity for a knowledge of *From Ritual to Romance* he says, 'Miss Weston is clearly a theosophist, and Mr. Eliot's poem might be a theosophical tract. The sick king and the waste land symbolise, we gather, the sick soul and the desolation of this material life.' Having gathered this correctly, Lucas seems perverse in looking on the poem as giving any suggestion of being a theosophical tract. The symbols are quite obviously used for their poetic value, with no suggestion that they have so specific and limited a meaning as Lucas suggests. That Lucas is not merely speaking ironically in saying this is indicated by his opinion that Eliot has 'sacrificed his artistic powers on the altar of some fantastic mumbo-jumbo'. Morosely he concludes, 'Perhaps this unhappy composition should have been left to sink itself.'

Whatever may be our opinion of the worth of these early criticisms it is undeniable that they deal with matters that must arise in any serious consideration of the poem. Despite the exhaustiveness of the commentaries by Leavis, Matthiessen, and Brooks, it will be necessary to give some account of the poem, as a basis on which speculation may rest. The following analysis is considerably indebted to the work of these critics. The conclusion, however, is somewhat different, and there are differences of detail.

Of greatest importance are the questions of the poem's unity, of the success of the system of allusion, and of the beliefs embodied in the work. This last is particularly interesting, for the general view of the poem is that it offers no evidence of positive belief, even that it has effected 'a complete severance between . . . poetry and all beliefs'—an interpretation which Eliot has professed himself unable to understand (*Selected Essays:* 'Dante', p. 269). The poem is not, as Day Lewis sees it, a social document. Nor is it an Act of Parliament setting forth exact instructions for the removal of evil conditions. But it does reveal a poetic treatment of certain aspects of a civilisation, placing them in the perspective of time.

Miss Weston's *From Ritual to Romance* is by now so well known /100/ as to require little comment. The Fisher King of the Grail legend having lost his virility through sexual mutilation or illness, his lands become waste and desolate, the power of propagation generally suspended. These ills are considered the direct result of the king's disability. On the success of the Quester in his task of journeying to the Grail chapel, there undergoing trials and ascertaining the office of the Grail and the significance of its symbols, depends the return of fertility to the land. Further, Weston distinguishes two parts of the legend, the esoteric and exoteric. The former concerns the significance of the Grail symbols. The latter gives the popular, folk-lore elements: the suffering king, the waste land, the task that lies before the Quester. It is this that Eliot uses. One can detect here the feeling for the spiritual condition of the large masses of humanity that prompts his introduction of Madame Blavatsky in 'A Cooking Egg'. Finally it must be noted that Eliot's use of Miss Weston's study involves an extension of the symbolism, found also in some of the legends, to cover not only physical but spiritual decay.

In the exoteric aspect of the legend, interest — as far as any hope of regeneration is concerned — must centre on the Quester's journey to the Grail chapel. Each of the five sections of *The Waste Land* introduces a journey undertaken by the inhabitants, generally a journey of no spiritual import, part of a social routine. Only in sections IV and V — 'Death by Water' (the voyage of the Phoenician sailor) and 'What the Thunder Said' — does the travelling assume any wider scope. The first three sections of the poem deal with what we may call the social realities of the waste land: with what its people see and do. This picture is illuminated by occasional flashes of insight on the part of some of the speakers, by the introduction of Tiresias, who comments on the action, and by the hidden commentary of the allusions to past literatures.

In the fifth part the emphasis changes and we are shown behind the social coverings to see directly the disease of the land and its people. It has entirely the atmosphere of nightmare, but this apparent fantasy probes beyond the earlier social reality to the basic issues of the poem. We remain conscious of the preceding background, but are aware now that it was partly responsible for concealing from the people the true nature of their position. /101/

*". . . The Dial has caused an explosion so splendid that [Eliot] . . .
'became the most significant poet in the English language of his
day."*

William Wasserstrom

HOW THE POEM APPEARED IN AMERICA

In 1919 when Sylvia Beach opened her bookshop in Paris as a
center for American expatriates, the guiding genius of national
life was not Whitman whose 1855 edition of *Leaves of Grass* Miss
Beach enshrined on permanent display. In Whitman's place there
was Arnold Rothstein who, arranging the outcome of the World
Series, engaged in a gambol of the moral life consistent in spirit
with the literary frivolities of *Smart Set* or *Vanity Fair.* Confronting
Rothstein, distressed by the transfer abroad of Whitman's spirit,
amused but displeased by the literary situation in America, two
wealthy young men, Scofield Thayer and J. S. Watson, Jr., in 1919
bought a magazine — *The Dial* — which for thirty-six years had been
published in Chicago as a model of taste in the Middle West. Once
sprightly but now staid ("the stationary part of a clock or other
chronometer," Ezra Pound said), in 1918 *The Dial* had been removed
to New York and reorganized as a magazine of politics. The board of
editors included John Dewey, Randolph Bourne, Thorstein Veblen
and Thayer, its patron. Then during the following year Watson and
Thayer turned it into a monthly magazine of letters and art.

By mid-decade their *Dial* had become the most influential
American journal of its kind. But by 1929 when Watson decided to

From "T. S. Eliot and *The Dial,*" *The Sewanee Review,* Vol. 70, No. 1 (Winter 1962), 81-92.
Copyright © 1962 by The University of the South. Reprinted by permission of the author and
publisher.

suspend publication, its influence had passed to other magazines in America and England, to *Hound and Horn, The Symposium, The Criterion.* Since that time two classic opinions have shaped its reputation. It's been called a pioneer but amateurish paper produced according to no particular policy—one of "those little magazines," William Phillips and Philip Rahv said in 1944, which flourished in the twenties and had "the good fortune of coming across such essentially *'new'* writing as . . . *The Waste Land* . . ." And it's been accused of having initiated what /81/ William Barrett sees as "the dangerous American tradition" of a purely literary paper. Barrett's view is sanctioned mainly by Van Wyck Brooks who decided long ago that this dangerous tradition was invented when *The Dial* published "The Waste Land." Embracing Eliot, it instituted the betrayal, both literary and social, which enabled Pound, John Crowe Ransom and Allen Tate to distract American writers from fulfillment of their proper tasks, from the creation of works that display Whitmanesque visions. Brooks' thought is succinct in William Carlos Williams' *Autobiography,* where we learn that *The Dial,* presenting Eliot's poem, "wiped out our world as if an atomic bomb had been dropped on it."

This quick sketch of the origins and reputation of *The Dial* is offered as a way of introducing a situation unique in American literary history. There is no other instance where a single work by one contributor has determined the worth of a journal which itself helped to shape the life of its time. Alone among the many magazines of the day, its nineteen volumes of fiction and verse, of criticism—in music, literature, painting and general culture—include contributions by every major modern writer in Europe and America. It alone offered reproductions, in color, of painting and sculpture by leading advanced artists. Only this magazine conferred an annual award on the best new American writers—and selected a peculiarly notable group: Sherwood Anderson, Eliot, Brooks, Marianne Moore, E. E. Cummings, Williams, Pound and Kenneth Burke. That the quality of this journal, itself unique, should be incorporated within the legend of Eliot's career is therefore extraordinary indeed. And now, as fierce men in England and the United States undertake to destroy the myth of Eliot, it is appropriate to return to that time when *The Dial,* introducing "The Waste Land," decided to sponsor Eliot's work. For that momentous event does not dramatize Thayer's decision to advance Eliot's plans. The amazing thing is that Thayer thought he was en- /82/ listing Eliot in his own cause, in *The Dial's* program for American letters and art.

II

Official association between journal and writer began in 1920 when Thayer appointed Eliot to serve as his correspondent from London. Assigning this job to Eliot, Thayer and Watson presented him with his first opportunity to speak freely on matters of personal and general interest to a large public at home and abroad. Hitherto, his work had been known only to a small group of friends and colleagues in London and New York. But by December, 1922, when Eliot resigned his post with *The Dial*, Watson and Thayer had published ten separate items (including "Ulysses, Order and Myth" and "The Waste Land"); presented him with The Dial Award, a grant of $2,000 for "service to American literature;" printed reviews of his work by E. E. Cummings, Marianne Moore, Edmund Wilson; and, in space reserved for the editors' own comment, proclaimed him the exemplary modern critic and poet. During its remaining years, even as Eliot's own *Criterion* enlarged its audience and its sphere of interest, *The Dial* published six additional pieces.*

Recalling these external signs of connection, we see right off why men of the twenties were accustomed to associate Eliot with *The Dial*. In order to clarify some abiding problems in literary history, however, we must refer to more subtle matters of biography and doctrine. For Thayer's own life and Eliot's had intersected at certain moments during their early years, at the /83/ Milton Academy, at Harvard and at Oxford, where they knew each other but weren't friends. Not only had Thayer been impressed by the elder boy's genius but also, perhaps coincidentally, he had very early adopted the principle which was to supply Eliot with a key idea for *The Sacred Wood*. There we learned to admire poets whose verse does not reveal a "dissociation of sensibility" because it is composed by men who "feel their thought as immediately as the odour of a rose." I've cited familiar phrases from a famous essay, "The Metaphysical Poets." Had I offered the reasons why Cummings, in *The Dial* for 1920, admired Eliot's first volume of verse, these would scarcely present a similar bouquet. But if we disregard Eliot's care-

*Among these is a version of "The Hollow Men" which, so far as I know, no specialist has studied. In *A Reader's Guide to T. S. Eliot,* George Williamson's standard work on problems of analysis and of text, "The Hollow Men" is described as "the first poem to illustrate the piecemeal composition and publication that have marked Eliot's longer poems since *The Waste Land.*" Mr. Williamson notes that "Part III appeared as the third item in another group called 'Doris's Dream Songs' . . . "; that only Part V was not published separately. But he doesn't specify another fact—that the poem Eliot printed in *The Dial* appeared without Parts IV and V. This version, which served as a kind of work-sheet for the final draft, makes no reference to the prickly pear, uses lines later extended and reserved for historic effect, ends without bang or whimper. /83/

fully wrought vocabulary, we realize that he and Cummings shared essentially the same opinion on the quality prime in art of the first rank: it must be intense. When a work is intense, Eliot and Cummings agreed, it provokes in the reader a heightened sense of his own being. Indeed, only when a work of art performs this act of provocation does it itself come fully to life. Cummings today says he has "no notion how Thayer evolved the idea that *art* is au fond intense (& unart isn't) but feel sure the idea first came to me from him." Miss Moore, too, who served as editor from 1925 until 1929, recalls this as the one principle which guided editorial decision: the word Thayer "reiterated oftenest . . . as a testing quality . . . was 'intensity'!"

The idea is not original with Thayer or Eliot, or even with Pound and T. E. Hulme, though all used this word. According to Meyer H. Abrams' study of nineteenth century ideas, *The Mirror and the Lamp*, the term has a history of its own which began when Longinus said that sublimity results from an inspired moment of passion. Longinus' thought reappears among the Romantics, mainly Keats and Coleridge, whose work led Carlyle and Poe and Arnold to adopt intensity itself as a leading idea of value in verse. Mr. Abrams does not refer to its next transmutation, to Pater's description of the flaming intensities of /84/ art, though this illumined the minds of esthetes at Oxford and Harvard. Before long, pragmatized and Americanized, it reappears in Bernard Berenson's system as the principle of life-enhancement: "a plunging into a state of being, or state of mind, that makes one feel not only physically alive but morally and spiritually as well; reaching out to the topmost peak of our capacities." Tracing the uses of intensity in the minds of Romantics from Keats to Berenson, we are not surprised to learn that Thayer and Eliot, trained at about the same time by a common group of teachers in the same schools, sought to find new ways to apply an old principle. For it is precisely this confluence of ideas which underlies Eliot's lifelong conviction that verse drama is the ideal form of literature because drama itself and verse rhythm "make for intensity." And in an age of diffusion "an hour and a half of *intense* interest" is exactly what the arts must recover.

Knowing that *The Dial's* policies and Eliot's poems were molded by this semi-systematic idea, we recognize why the tone of Eliot's verse especially pleased Thayer's ear. But Thayer's support of Eliot's career was rooted in still higher, more public ground – in the very ground, indeed, where Brooks stood alongside his friend, Randolph Bourne. In 1918 Bourne had written a series of essays in which he had argued that Americans will "never be able to perpetuate [their] ideals except in the form of art and literature." That year, too, when Thayer persuaded Watson to help him finance a journal which would serve as a vehicle for Bourne's ideas, it was decided to install Bourne as editor. Bourne's death in 1918 forced Thayer to modify his procedure but not to change his program. Although he and Watson altered the shape of *The Dial*, they did not shift its purpose. And a fortnightly journal which had been preoccupied by the politics of utopia became a monthly magazine absorbed in the arts of utopia.

Neither Thayer nor Watson was a chauvinist, however, and both had grown impatient with earlier efforts to achieve similar goals—with the stridencies and parochialism of taste in *The Seven* /85/ *Arts*. Describing Bourne as the genius of the Seven Arts Group, Watson said its members—Brooks, Paul Rosenfeld, James Oppenheim and Waldo Frank—were inclined to "despise as unAmerican very admirable and very American poets like Ezra Pound, Marianne Moore, and William Carlos Williams." Watson was convinced that Williams especially should be encouraged because he knew "what the United States needs in order to ripen a literature." To Watson's list Thayer added Eliot's name. Watson himself had decided that Eliot's criticism helped to clarify and rearrange ideas in "the same surprising way as do . . . Freud's theories of sex in childhood." But Thayer was certain—however strange today his certainty may seem—that Eliot was in fact the savior they'd all been waiting for. Alone among American poets he was not victimized by that "'localism' which . . . takes so much of American writing out of the field of comparison with European letters" and requires for our writers a "special standard of judgement." By 1922, therefore, both Thayer and Watson had selected Eliot as the man who might fulfill historic aims of art and life in America, the sort of writer whom Whitman and Brooks and Bourne had said must be encouraged if America were ever to make its spirit count in the great world of art and affairs.

Not until the mid-twenties did Thayer realize that Eliot was moved by private motives of another kind. At that time he felt less and less sympathy for a poet whose new subject and manner he couldn't follow; for an editor who ran a rival magazine that once or twice condescended to say a word of praise about *The Dial*. In 1925, no longer enchanted by Eliot and prepared to resign as editor, he offered his post to Brooks but was refused. He didn't mention to Watson either his own offer or Brooks' refusal. And since Brooks was asked not to publicize the invitation, it remained unknown until 1958 when he told Gilbert Seldes who mentioned the matter to me. Later, responding to my note, Brooks said, "Yes, I was offered the editorship . . . but I was at the moment at the beginning of a serious nervous /86/ breakdown and could not have accepted the offer. Besides I was no longer interested in editing a magazine. Mr. Scofield Thayer asked me at the time not to mention this, but as it is now more than thirty years ago I see no reason for keeping this a secret." Thayer did say publicly that he believed Brooks to be a man of "supreme importance" even though he could not accept "the whole body" of Brooks' doctrine. Offering this particular critic the most powerful literary post in New York, Thayer hoped to furnish Bourne's old friend with a magazine which would enable him to establish his American School of art—that School for which in *Letters and Leadership* Brooks had made so fervent a case.

Until mid-decade, however, Thayer was convinced that Eliot was the white hope of letters. And in 1922 when "The Waste Land" arrived, he was certain the time had come for major celebration. The poem itself disappointed him: he thought it was not so good as Eliot's earlier verse. Watson insisted it was a master work. Thayer was unconvinced but he had already decided to present Eliot with The Dial Award for 1922. Beginning in August, the staff made careful plans. "With Liveright I have arranged as follows," the managing editor, Gilbert Seldes, told Watson: "We pay them nothing and we publish the poem without the notes in our November issue. They bring out the book after our date of publication and we send them an order for 350 copies at our usual discount . . . We take the entire lot of 350 by January 1st and make financial settlement by that time. (The idea, of course, is that we will push the book mightily in connection with our subscriptions. The book sells for $2. so that if it remains a total loss on our hands we will be paying about $350.) I have suggested that they number all the copies of the first edition, giving a bibliographical value to it, and they have promised to use no publicity mentioning the award until we release it." Turning next to the poem itself, Seldes remarked that "We must assume that Eliot O.K.'s publication in *The Dial* without the /87/ notes . . . which are exceedingly interesting and add much to the poem, but don't become interested in them because we simply cannot have them."

These issues settled, the Editors next tried to find a critic whose opinion would help readers to decide in the poet's favor. They wanted a man of reputation who would write a notice: serious criticism would come later. But they would not settle for an essay which wasn't worthy of its subject. Early in October Seldes wrote to George Saintsbury about their plan to publish the poem and confer the Award. "Because Eliot's poetry is not widely known," he said, "we plan to present an essay upon his work. We would like this essay to come from you." Saintsbury refused. Watson's first choice was Pound but he knew that Thayer would not agree. Then he thought that perhaps Padraic Colum, whom he admired and who "can write fair criticism" which pleases "the conservatives and 'poetry lovers'," might be the right man. Earlier Edmund Wilson had offered to write a critical essay and, pressed by time, Watson said finally that "it will be ok to let Wilson" do the review.

To publish Wilson, another little known American writer, was to compound the gamble. But his study, "The Poetry of Drouth," didn't embarrass them at all: like all his subsequent work, its learning was subdued but sure, its exposition and judgment were deft. This essay capped *The Dial's* effort to introduce a poet whose "trivialities are more valuable than other people's epics." Although Eliot's poems are "the products of a constricted emotional experience," Wilson said, the work of a man who "appears to have drawn rather heavily on books for the heat he could not derive from life," nevertheless Eliot's "detestation of Sweeney is more precious than Mr. Sandburg's sympathy for him." And when next month Thayer announced that "for the year 1922 *The Dial's* Award goes to Mr. T. S. Eliot," he was unmistakably pleased by his triumph. For he had just read "the most influential editor-critic in London" and discovered that the man had /88/ "found nothing to say" about "The Waste Land" except that it was an "obscure but amusing poem." Thayer suggested that his readers compare Wilson's essay—later revised for *Axel's Castle*—with the other, the American reception with the English, in order that they might "judge of the state of criticism in England." What he did not know, of course, was that *The Dial* had caused an explosion so splendid that echoes of the great event would continue to return from remote places even in 1960 when, in Enid Starkie's study of French influences on English writing, we hear that Eliot, "awarded by *The Dial* . . . their poetry prize for his *Wasteland* . . . became the most significant poet in the English language of his day."

III

One last word must be said before this inquiry ends. In that moment when poet and paper coalesce, we recognize a fulfillment

of motives which in 1919 had led Watson and Thayer to refurb-
ish their magazine. And recognition in turn compels us to modify
the work of historians who have misled us, who have misconstrued
the moods common among American men of letters after the War.
Like Alfred Kazin who in *On Native Grounds* mistook a general
disavowal of politics for total disenchantment with dreams of
utopia — like Kazin, we have tended to think that "nothing was so
dead in 1920" as "the crusading spirit of 1910."

Surely that moment of coalescence could not have occurred if
Thayer had not sought to invoke precisely this spirit. Had the poem,
unattended by Wilson's essay or *The Dial's* Award, appeared in
The Little Review or *Poetry,* its effect would doubtless have been
neither more nor less stunning than in London during October when
it came out in the first number of the *Criterion.* Had there been no
Award, there'd have been no essay. Both Award and essay — like
poem and journal — represent main aspects of Thayer's program,
and Thayer's program itself manifests aims which contradict
Kazin's idea. That is to say, *The Dial's* crusade in Eliot's behalf is
identical in spirit with Thayer's /89/ crusade in behalf of American
letters. And it is nothing less than the crusading spirit of 1910
that had by 1922 conferred on this journal its peculiar power.

"Thirty thousand readers," Thayer announced in November,
1923, and "every new subscriber . . . a participant in the success
of *The Dial* — a success which is making artistic history. Join this
group . . . of pioneers, and identify yourself with this country's
art and letters. . . ." "To distinguish the delicate from the fragile,
the exquisite from the unusual, the imaginative from the fanciful,
the original from the eccentric; to whip the *crème de la crème* from
the milk-pails of the Elysian Fields; to astonish the stupid, to
bewilder the clever, to stimulate the intelligent, to satisfy the
intellectual, such . . . is the rôle of the famous *Dial* of the 'twenties.'" "GROW WITH THE DIAL" "Future Historians of the Art
and Literature of America will . . . point to *The Dial*" as the most
distinguished achievement of the age. Answering complaints from
American contributors who wondered how the appearance of
foreign writers accomplished these aims, Thayer said that he published Europeans as colleagues who participate in the "Western-
civilized-Christian-European-American-tradition." In this tradition
each literature maintains its "independent existence," its "separate,
precious character," its uniqueness within the community as a
whole. Although he didn't identify the source of this idea, we can
trace it to Bourne's vision of America as the place where men have
managed to achieve "that miracle . . . the peaceful living side by

side, with character substantially preserved, of the most heterogeneous people" on earth. Bourne was certain that America was
destined to fulfill historic prophecies because these States alone
had contrived to establish a "world federation in miniature,"
that international community for which all civilized men yearn.
Thayer, applying this principle not to politics but to art, made *The
Dial* a symbol of what Bourne called trans-nationality. Publishing
"The Waste Land," he publicized both the uniqueness of American
writing and its /90/ authority. November, 1922, was a signal moment in the history of the world, Thayer half-playfully believed, for
then it was that this journal and this poet and this national literature assumed their proper role: first among equals in the republic of
letters.

"I'd say," Eliot in 1959 told an interviewer for *The Paris Review*, that "my poetry has obviously more in common with my
distinguished contemporaries in America than with anything
written in my generation in England. . . ." In its "emotional
springs it comes from America." Eliot is modest. We must include
not his poetry alone but his whole achievement as well, not springs
merely but program too. A man reared within a native utopian
tradition, taught to admire only those intense works which bring
an audience to life, Eliot has written a continental literature in
the American grain. For he, Brooks, Williams, Pound, Thayer
and Watson — all members of this generation hoped to shape civilization according to the model presented by art. All sought somehow
to perform a ritual which would unite play, player and public,
writer and reader, journal and audience, much as "the working
man who went to a music hall and saw Marie Lloyd and joined in
the chorus was performing part of the work of acting; he was
engaging in that collaboration of the audience with the artist,
which is necessary in all art. . . ." These remarks, which Eliot
was to incorporate in his famed essay on the British music-hall
artist, were first printed in his London Letter for *The Dial* in
December, 1922.

Exactly the same values Eliot imagined were visible in Marie
Lloyd, Thayer and Watson were certain Eliot's own verse displayed. Here at last was an American writer who would help his
countrymen find what he himself found in English music halls —
"the artistic expression and dignity of their own lives." When
poem and public join, when "The Waste Land" infuses America,
when *Dial* and Dream blend, then ordinary men are inspired to re-
make their lives. Inspired so, men might reclaim national life /91/
from the control of Arnold Rothstein — from the control, as Thayer

himself remarked, of those "twin shrunken Caesars," President Calvin C. Coolidge and Bishop William T. Manning. For this most ardent of crusaders believed that he had fashioned a journal in which American artists, guaranteed a public, would at last create that moment of apocalypse when, as Whitman had prophesied, a land redeemed by art would save the world.

And now, forty years late, realizing that *The Dial* presented "The Waste Land" as a peculiar amalgam of intensity and propheticism, of Scofield Thayer and Randolph Bourne, we are compelled to recognize Eliot's poem as the work which best identifies the inner life of a magazine designed to interlace American art and civilization. /92/

part 2

SOME EARLY CRITICS

Eliot's "trick of cutting his corners and his curves makes him seem obscure when he is clear as daylight. His thoughts move very rapidly and by astounding cuts. They move not by logical stages and majestic roundings of the full literary curve, but as live thoughts move in live brains."

May Sinclair, quoted by Edmund Wilson, *Axel's Castle* (New York, 1931), p. 108

"The rich disorganization of the poem [attempts] to focus an inclusive human consciousness. . . . [The organization] may, by analogy, be called musical."

F. R. Leavis

THE POEM'S UNITY

It was *The Waste Land* that compelled recognition for Eliot's achievement. The poem appeared first in the opening numbers of *The Criterion* (October 1922 and January 1923). The title, we know, comes from Miss J. L. Weston's book, *From Ritual to Romance,* the theme of which is anthropological: the Waste Land there has a significance in terms of Fertility Ritual. What is the significance of the modern Waste Land? The answer may be read in what appears as the rich disorganization of the poem. The seeming disjointedness is intimately related to the erudition that has annoyed so many readers[1] and to the /90/ wealth of literary borrowings and allusions. These characteristics reflect the present state of civilization. The

From *New Bearings in English Poetry* by F. R. Leavis (London: Chatto & Windus, Ltd., 1950), Chapter III, "T. S. Eliot," pp. 90-114. Originally published in 1932. Published in the United States in 1960 by the University of Michigan Press, Ann Arbor, and reprinted by their permission.

[1]'I don't like his erudition-traps,' said a very distinguished author to me once. And this, from *Gallion's Reach* (pp. 35-36), by H. M. Tomlinson, is representative:

'His grin broadened. "All I can say is, my dear, give me the old /90/ songs, though I can't sing them, if they're the new. What does poetry want with footnotes about psycho-analysis and negro mythology?"

'"Suppose," someone asked him, "that you don't know anything about them?"

'"Well, I couldn't get them out of footnotes and the poetry all at one stride, could I? But Doris, they were very clever and insulting poems, I think. Sing a song of mockery. Is that the latest? But it was a surprising little book, though it smelt like the dissection of bad innards."'

The novelist, with a certain subtle naïveté, clearly identifies himself with the attitude, and he clearly means the reader to do the same. And there is every reason to suppose that he would not object to the reader's supposing that he had Mr Eliot in mind. The First Edition of *Gallion's Reach* is valuable. /91/

traditions and cultures have mingled, and the historical imagination makes the past contemporary; no one tradition can digest so great a variety of materials, and the result is a break-down of forms and the irrevocable loss of that sense of absoluteness which seems necessary to a robust culture. The bearing of this on the technique developed in *Burbank* and *A Cooking Egg* does not need enlarging upon.

In considering our present plight we have also to take account of the incessant rapid change that characterizes the Machine Age. The result is breach of continuity and the uprooting of life. This last metaphor has a peculiar aptness, for what we are witnessing to-day is the final uprooting of the immemorial ways of life, of life rooted in the soil. The urban imagery that affiliates /91/ Mr Eliot to Baudelaire and Laforgue has its significance; a significance that we touched on in glancing at the extreme contrast between Mr Eliot and Hardy. We may take Mr T. F. Powys to-day as the successor of Hardy: he is probably the last considerable artist of the old order (he seems to me a great one). It does not seem likely that it will ever again be possible for a distinguished mind to be formed, as Mr Powys has been, on the rhythms, sanctioned by nature and time, of rural culture. The spirit of *Mr Weston's Good Wine* could not be described as one of traditional faith; all the more striking, then, is the contrast in effect between Mr Powys's and Mr Eliot's preoccupation with 'birth, copulation and death.'[1] Mr Powys's disillusion belongs to the old world, and the structure and organization of his art are according. There is no need to elaborate the comparison.

The remoteness of the civilization celebrated in *The Waste Land* from the natural rhythms is brought out, in ironical contrast, by the anthropo- /92/ logical theme. Vegetation cults, fertility ritual, with their sympathetic magic, represent a harmony of human culture with the natural environment, and express an extreme sense of the unity of life. In the modern Waste Land

> April is the cruellest month, breeding
> Lilacs out of the dead land,

[1]
> Nothing at all but three things
> DORIS.   What things?
> SWEENEY. Birth, copulation, and death.
> That's all, that's all, that's all, that's all.
> Birth, copulation, and death.
> DORIS.   I'd be bored
> SWEENEY.   You'd be bored.
> Birth, copulation, and death.'
> *Fragment of an Agon. Criterion*, Jan. 1927. /92/

but bringing no quickening to the human spirit. Sex here is sterile, breeding not life and fulfilment but disgust, accidia and unanswerable questions. It is not easy to-day to accept the perpetuation and multiplication of life as ultimate ends.

But the anthropological background has positive functions. It plays an obvious part in evoking that particular sense of the unity of life which is essential to the poem. It helps to establish the level of experience at which the poem works, the mode of consciousness to which it belongs. In *The Waste Land* the development of impersonality that *Gerontion* shows in comparison with *Prufrock* reaches an extreme limit: it would be difficult to imagine a completer transcendence of the individual self, a completer projection of awareness. We have, in the introductory chapter, considered the poet as being at the conscious point of his age. There are ways in which it is possible to be too conscious; and to be so is, as a result of the break-up of forms and the loss of axioms noted /93/ above, one of the troubles of the present age (if the abstraction may be permitted, consciousness being in any case a minority affair). We recognize in modern literature the accompanying sense of futility.

The part that science in general has played in the process of disintegration is matter of commonplace: anthropology is, in the present context, a peculiarly significant expression of the scientific spirit. To the anthropological eye beliefs, religions and moralities are human habits—in their odd variety too human. Where the anthropological outlook prevails, sanctions wither. In a contemporary consciousness there is inevitably a great deal of the anthropological, and the background of *The Waste Land* is thus seen to have a further significance.

To be, then, too much conscious and conscious of too much—that is the plight:

After such knowledge, what forgiveness?

At this point Mr Eliot's note[1] on Tiresias deserves attention:

Tiresias, although a mere spectator and not indeed a 'character,' is yet the most important personage in the poem, uniting all the rest. Just as the one-eyed merchant, seller of currants, melts into the Phoenician Sailor, and the latter is not wholly distinct from Ferdinand Prince of Naples, so all the /94/ women

[1]Note to line 218 of *The Waste Land* (*Poems* 1909-1925, p. 88). /94/

are one woman, and the two sexes meet in Tiresias. What Tiresias *sees,* in fact, is the substance of the poem.

If Mr Eliot's readers have a right to a grievance, is it that he has not given this note more salience; for it provides the clue to *The Waste Land.* It indicates plainly enough what the poem is: an effort to focus an inclusive human consciousness. The effort, in ways suggested above, is characteristic of the age; and in an age of psycho-analysis, an age that has produced the last section of *Ulysses,* Tiresias—'venus huic erat utraque nota'—presents himself as the appropriate impersonation. A cultivated modern is (or feels himself to be) intimately aware of the experience of the opposite sex.

Such an undertaking offers a difficult problem of organization, a distinguishing character of the mode of consciousness that pro-motes it being a lack of organizing principle, the absence of any inherent direction. A poem that is to contain all myths cannot con-struct itself upon one. It is here that *From Ritual to Romance* comes in. It provides a background of reference that makes possible some-thing in the nature of a musical[1] organization. Let us start by con-sidering the use of the Tarot pack. Introduced in the first section, /95/ suggesting, as it does, destiny, chance and the eternal mysteries, it at once intimates the scope of the poem, the mode of its contem-plation of life. It informs us as to the nature of the characters: we know that they are such as could not have relations with one another in any narrative scheme, and could not be brought together on any stage, no matter what liberties were taken with the Unities. The immediate function of the passage introducing the pack, more-over, is to evoke, in contrast with what has preceded, cosmopolitan 'high life,' and the charlatanism that battens upon it:

Madame Sosostris, famous clairvoyante,
Had a bad cold, nevertheless
Is known to be the wisest woman in Europe,
With a wicked pack of cards.

Mr Eliot can achieve the banality appropriate here, and achieve at the same time, when he wants it, a deep undertone, a resonance, as it were, of fate:

. . . and this card,
Which is blank, is something he carries on his back,

---

[1]Mr I. A. Richards uses the analogy from music in some valuable notes on Mr Eliot that are printed in an appendix to the later editions of *The Principles of Literary Criticism.* /95/

Which I am forbidden to see. I do not find
The Hanged Man. Fear death by water.
I see crowds of people, walking round in a ring.

The peculiar menacing undertone of this associates it with a passage
in the fifth section:

Who is the third who walks always beside you?
When I count, there are only you and I together /96/
But when I look ahead up the white road
There is always another one walking beside you
Gliding wrapt in a brown mantle, hooded
I do not know whether a man or a woman
—But who is that on the other side of you?

The association establishes itself without any help from Mr Eliot's
note; it is there in any case, as any fit reader of poetry can report;
but the note helps us to recognize its significance:

The Hanged Man, a member of the traditional pack, fits my
purpose in two ways: because he is associated in my mind with
the Hanged God of Frazer, and because I associate him with the
hooded figure in the passage of the disciples to Emmaus in
Part V.

The Tarot pack, Miss Weston has established, has affiliations
with fertility ritual, and so lends itself peculiarly to Mr Eliot's
purpose: the instance before us illustrates admirably how he has
used its possibilities. The hooded figure in the passage just quoted
is Jesus. Perhaps our being able to say so depends rather too much
upon Mr Eliot's note; but the effect of the passage does not depend
so much upon the note as might appear. For Christ has figured
already in the opening of the section (see *What the Thunder Said*):

After the torchlight red on sweaty faces
After the frosty silence in the gardens
After the agony in stony places /97/
The shouting and the crying
Prison and palace and reverberation
Of thunder of spring over distant mountains
He who was living is now dead
We who were living are now dying
With a little patience

The reference is unmistakable. Yet it is not only Christ; it is also the Hanged God and all the sacrificed gods: with the 'thunder of spring' 'Adonis, Attis, Osiris' and all the others of *The Golden Bough* come in. And the 'agony in stony places' is not merely the Agony in the Garden; it is also the agony of the Waste Land, introduced in the first section: (*The Burial of the Dead*, ll. 19 ff.).

> What are the roots that clutch, what branches grow
> Out of this stony rubbish? Son of man,
> You cannot say, or guess, for you know only
> A heap of broken images, where the sun beats,
> And the dead tree gives no shelter, the cricket no relief,
> And the dry stone no sound of water.

In *What the Thunder Said* the drouth becomes (among other things) a thirst for the waters of faith and healing, and the specifically religious enters into the orchestration of the poem. But the thunder is 'dry sterile thunder without rain'; there is no resurrection or renewal; and after the opening passage the verse loses all buoyancy, and /98/ takes on a dragging, persistent movement as of hopeless exhaustion—

> Here is no water but only rock
> Rock and no water and the sandy road
> The road winding above among the mountains
> Which are mountains of rock without water

—the imagined sound of water coming in as a torment. There is a suggestion of fever here, a sultry ominousness—

> There is not even solitude in the mountains

—and it is this which provides the transition to the passage about the hooded figure quoted above. The ominous tone of this last passage associates it, as we have seen, with the reference (ll. 55-56) to the Hanged Man in the Tarot passage of *The Burial of the Dead*. So Christ becomes the Hanged Man, the Vegetation God; and at the same time the journey through the Waste Land along 'the sandy road' becomes the Journey to Emmaus. Mr Eliot gives us a note on the 'third who walks always beside you':   →32

The following lines were stimulated by the account of one of the Antarctic expeditions (I forget which, but I think one of

Shackleton's): it was related that the party of explorers, at the extremity of their strength, had the constant delusion that there was *one more member* than could actually be counted.

This might be taken to be, from our point of view, merely an interesting irrelevance, and it /99/ certainly is not necessary. But it nevertheless serves to intimate the degree of generality that Mr Eliot intends to accompany his concrete precision: he is both definite and vague at once. 'Just as the one-eyed merchant, seller of currants, melts into the Phoenician Sailor, and the latter is not wholly distinct from Ferdinand Prince of Naples' — so one experience is not wholly distinct from another experience of the same general order; and just as all experiences 'meet in Tiresias,' so a multitude of experiences meet in each passage of the poem. Thus the passage immediately in question has still further associations. That same hallucinatory quality which relates it to what goes before recalls also the neurasthenic episode (ll. III ff.) in *A Game of Chess* (the second section):

'What is that noise?'
          The wind under the door.
'What is that noise now? . . .'

All this illustrates the method of the poem, and the concentration, the depth of orchestration that Mr Eliot achieves; the way in which the themes move in and out of one another and the predominance shifts from level to level. The transition from this passage is again by way of the general ominousness, which passes into hallucinated vision and then into nightmare: /100/

—But who is that on the other side of you?

What is that sound high in the air
Murmur of maternal lamentation
Who are those hooded hordes swarming
Over endless plains, stumbling in cracked earth
Ringed by the flat horizon only
What is the city over the mountains
Cracks and reforms and bursts in the violet air
Falling towers
Jerusalem Athens Alexandria
Vienna London
Unreal.

The focus of attention shifts here to the outer disintegration in its
large, obvious aspects, and the references to Russia and to post-war
Europe in general are plain. The link between the hooded figure of
the road to Emmaus and the 'hooded hordes swarming' is not much
more than verbal (though appropriate to a fevered consciousness),
but this phrase has an essential association with a line (56) in the
passage that introduces the Tarot pack:

I see crowds of people walking round in a ring.

These 'hooded hordes,' 'ringed by the flat horizon only,' are not
merely Russians, suggestively related to the barbarian invaders
of civilization; they are also humanity walking endlessly round in
a ring, a further illustration of the eternal futility. 'Unreal' picks
up the 'Unreal city' of *The Burial of the Dead* (l. 60), where 'Saint
/101/ Mary Woolnoth kept the hours,' and the unreality gets further
development in the nightmare passage that follows:

And upside down in air were towers
Tolling reminiscent bells, that kept the hours
And voices singing out of empty cisterns and exhausted wells.

Then, with a transitional reference (which will be commented
on later) to the theme of the Chapel Perilous, the focus shifts in-
wards again. 'Datta,' 'dayadhvam,' and 'damyata,' the admonitions
of the thunder, are explained in a note, and in this case, at any rate,
the reliance upon the note justifies itself. We need only be told once
that they mean 'give, sympathize, control,' and the context pre-
serves the meaning. The Sanscrit lends an appropriate portentousness, intimating that this is the sum of wisdom according to a great
tradition, and that what we have here is a radical scrutiny into the
profit of life. The irony, too, is radical:

Datta: what have we given?
My friend, blood shaking my heart
The awful daring of a moment's surrender
Which an age of prudence can never retract
By this, and this only, we have existed
. . . .

—it is an equivocal comment. And for comment on 'sympathize' we
have a reminder of the irremediable isolation of the individual.

After all /102/ the agony of sympathetic transcendence, it is to the individual, the focus of consciousness, that we return:

> Shall I at least set my lands in order?

The answer comes in the bundle of fragments that ends the poem, and, in a sense, sums it up.

Not that the *poem* lacks organization and unity. The frequent judgments that it does betray a wrong approach. The author of *The Lyric Impulse in the Poetry of T. S. Eliot,* for instance, speaks of 'a definitely willed attempt to weld various fine fragments into a metaphysical whole.' But the unity of *The Waste Land* is no more 'metaphysical' than it is narrative or dramatic, and to try to elucidate it metaphysically reveals complete misunderstanding. The unity the poem aims at is that of an inclusive consciousness: the organization it achieves as a work of art is of the kind that has been illustrated, an organization that may, by analogy, be called musical. It exhibits no progression:

> I sat upon the shore
> Fishing, with the arid plain behind me

—the thunder brings no rain to revive the Waste Land, and the poem ends where it began.

At this point the criticism has to be met that, while all this may be so, the poem in any case exists, and can exist, only for an extremely limited /103/ public equipped with special knowledge. The criticism must be admitted. But that the public for it is limited is one of the symptoms of the state of culture that produced the poem. Works expressing the finest consciousness of the age in which the word 'high-brow' has become current are almost inevitably such as to appeal only to a tiny minority.[1] It is still more serious that this minority should be more and more cut off from the world around it—should, indeed, be aware of a hostile and overwhelming environment. This amounts to an admission that there must be something limited about the kind of artistic achievement possible in our time: even Shakespeare in such conditions could hardly have been the 'universal' genius. And *The Waste Land,* clearly, is not of the order of *The Divine Comedy* or of *Lear.* The important admission, then, is not that *The Waste Land* can be appreciated only by a very small

[1]This matter is discussed at length by the present author in *Mass Civilisation and Minority Culture* (see *For Continuity*). /104/

minority (how large in any age has the minority been that has really comprehended the masterpieces?), but that this limitation carries with it limitations in self-sufficiency.

These limitations, however, are easily overstressed. Most of the 'special knowledge,' dependence upon which is urged against *The Waste Land,* can fairly be held to be common to /104/ the public that would in any case read modern poetry. The poem does, indeed, to some extent lean frankly upon *From Ritual to Romance.* And sometimes it depends upon external support in ways that can hardly be justified. Let us take, for instance, the end of the third section, *The Fire Sermon:*

> la la

> To Carthage then I came

> Burning, burning, burning, burning
> O Lord Thou pluckest me out
> O Lord Thou pluckest

> burning

It is plain from Mr Eliot's note on this passage — 'The collocation of these two representatives of eastern and western asceticism, as the culmination of this part of the poem, is not an accident' — that he intends St Augustine and the Buddha to be actively present here. But whereas one cursory reading of *From Ritual to Romance* does all (practically) that is assigned as function to that book, no amount of reading of the *Confessions* or *Buddhism in Translation* will give these few words power to evoke the kind of presence of 'eastern and western asceticism' that seems necessary to the poem: they remain, these words, mere pointers to something outside. We can only conclude that Mr Eliot here has not done as much /105/ as he supposes. And so with the passage (ll. 385 ff.) in *What the Thunder Said* bringing in the theme of the Chapel Perilous: it leaves too much to Miss Weston; repeated recourse to *From Ritual to Romance* will not invest it with the virtue it would assume. The irony, too, of the

> Shantih   shantih   shantih

that ends the poem is largely ineffective, for Mr Eliot's note that '"The Peace which passeth understanding" is a feeble translation of the content of this word' can impart to the word only a feeble ghost of that content for the Western reader.

Yet the weaknesses of this kind are not nearly as frequent or as damaging as critics of *The Waste Land* seem commonly to suppose. It is a self-subsistent poem, and should be obviously such. The allusions, references and quotations usually carry their own power with them as well as being justified in the appeal they make to special knowledge. 'Unreal City' (l. 60), to take an extreme instance from one end of the scale, owes nothing to Baudelaire (whatever Mr Eliot may have owed); the note is merely interesting — though, of course, it is probable that a reader unacquainted with Baudelaire will be otherwise unqualified. The reference to Dante that follows —

A crowd flowed over London Bridge, so many,
I had not thought death had undone so many /106/

— has an independent force, but much is lost to the reader who does not catch the implied comparison between London and Dante's Hell. Yet the requisite knowledge of Dante is a fair demand. The knowledge of *Antony and Cleopatra* assumed in the opening of *A Game of Chess*, or of *The Tempest* in various places elsewhere, no one will boggle at. The main references in *The Waste Land* come within the classes represented by these to Dante and Shakespeare; while of the many others most of the essential carry enough of their power with them. By means of such references and quotations Mr Eliot attains a compression, otherwise unattainable, that is essential to his aim; a compression approaching simultaneity — the co-presence in the mind of a number of different orientations, fundamental attitudes, orders of experience.

This compression and the methods it entails do make the poem difficult reading at first, and a full response comes only with familiarity. Yet the complete rout so often reported, or inadvertently revealed — as, for instance, by the critic who assumes that *The Waste Land* is meant to be a 'metaphysical whole' — can be accounted for only by a wrong approach, an approach with inappropriate expectations. For the general nature and method of the poem should be obvious at first reading. Yet so commonly does the obvious /107/ seem to be missed that perhaps a little more elucidation (this time of the opening section) will not be found offensively superfluous. What follows is a brief analysis of *The Burial of the Dead*, the avowed intention being to point out the obvious themes and transitions: anything like a full analysis would occupy many times the space.

The first seven lines introduce the vegetation theme, associating it with the stirring of 'memory and desire.' The transition is simple: 'April,' 'spring,' 'winter,'—then

> Summer surprised us, coming over the Starnbergersee
> With a shower of rain . . .

We seem to be going straight forward, but (as the change of movement intimates) we have modulated into another plane. We are now given a particular 'memory,' and a representative one. It introduces the cosmopolitan note, a note of empty sophistication:

> In the mountains, there you feel free.
> I read, much of the night, and go south in the winter.
> [Cf. 'Winter kept us warm']

The next transition is a contrast and a comment, bringing this last passage into relation with the first. April may stir dull roots with spring rain, but

> What are the roots that clutch, what branches grow
> Out of this stony rubbish? /108/

And there follows an evocation of the Waste Land, with references to *Ezekiel* and *Ecclesiastes,* confirming the tone that intimates that this is an agony of the soul ('Son of man' relates with the Hanged Man and the Hanged God: with him 'who was living' and 'is now dead' at the opening of *What the Thunder Said*). The 'fear'—

> I will show you fear in a handful of dust

—recurs, in different modes, in the neurasthenic passage (ll. III ff.) of *A Game of Chess,* and in the episode of the hooded figure in *What the Thunder Said.* The fear is partly the fear of death, but still more a nameless, ultimate fear, a horror of the completely negative.

Then comes the verse from *Tristan und Isolde,* offering a positive in contrast—the romantic absolute, love. The 'hyacinth girl,' we may say, represents 'memory and desire' (the hyacinth, directly evocative like the lilacs bred out of the Waste Land, was also one of the flowers associated with the slain vegetation god), and the 'nothing' of the Waste Land changes into the ecstasy of passion—a contrast, and something more:

—Yet when we came back, late, from the Hyacinth garden,
Your arms full, and your hair wet, I could not
Speak, and my eyes failed, I was neither
Living nor dead, and I knew nothing,
Looking into the heart of light, the silence. /109/

In the Waste Land one is neither living nor dead. Moreover, the
neurasthenic passage referred to above recalls these lines unmistakably, giving them a sinister modulation:

'Speak to me. Why do you never speak. Speak.
'What are you thinking of? What thinking? What?
'I never know what you are thinking. Think.'
. . . .
                              'Do
'You know nothing? Do you see nothing? Do you remember
'Nothing?'

The further line from *Tristan und Isolde* ends the passage of
romantic love with romantic desolation. Madame Sosostris, famous
clairvoyante, follows; she brings in the demi-monde, so offering a
further contrast—

Here is Belladonna, the Lady of the Rocks,
The lady of situations

—and introduces the Tarot pack. This passage has already received
some comment, and it invites a great deal more. The 'lady of situations,' to make an obvious point, appears in the *Game of Chess*.
The admonition, 'Fear death by water,' gets its response in the
fourth section, *Death by Water*: death is inevitable, and the life-
giving water thirsted for (and the water out of which all life comes)
cannot save. But enough has been said to indicate the function of
the Tarot pack, /110/ the way in which it serves in the organization
of the poem.

With the 'Unreal City' the background of urban—of 'megalo-
politan'—civilization becomes explicit. The allusion to Dante has
already been remarked upon, and so has the way in which Saint
Mary Woolnoth is echoed by the 'reminiscent bells' of *What the
Thunder Said*. The portentousness of the 'dead sound on the final
stroke of nine' serves as a transition, and the unreality of the City

turns into the intense but meaningless horror, the absurd inconse-
quence, of a nightmare:

> There I saw one I knew, and stopped him, crying: 'Stetson!
> 'You who were with me in the ships at Mylae!
> 'That corpse you planted last year in your garden,
> 'Has it begun to sprout? Will it bloom this year? . . .'

These last two lines pick up again the opening theme. The corpse
acquires a kind of nightmare association with the slain god of *The
Golden Bough,* and is at the same time a buried memory. Then, after
a reference to Webster (Webster's sepulchral horrors are robust),
The Burial of the Dead ends with the line in which Baudelaire,
having developed the themes of

> La sottise, l'erreur, le péché, la lésine

and finally *L'Ennui,* suddenly turns upon the /111/ reader to remind
him that he is something more.

The way in which *The Waste Land* is organized, then, should
be obvious even without the aid of notes. And the poet's mastery
should be as apparent in the organization as in the parts (where it
has been freely acclaimed). The touch with which he manages his
difficult transitions, his delicate collocations, is exquisitely sure.
His tone, in all its subtle variations, exhibits a perfect control. If
there is any instance where this last judgment must be qualified,
it is perhaps here (from the first passage of *The Fire Sermon*):

> Sweet Thames, run softly till I end my song,
> Sweet Thames, run softly, for I speak not loud or long.
> But at my back in a cold blast I hear
> The rattle of the bones, and chuckle spread from ear to ear.

These last two lines seem to have too much of the caricature quality
of *Prufrock* to be in keeping—for a certain keeping is necessary
(and Mr. Eliot commonly maintains it) even in contrasts. But even
if the comment is just, the occasion for it is a very rare exception.

The Waste Land, then, whatever its difficulty, is or should be,
obviously a poem.[1] It is a self- /112/ subsistent poem. Indeed, though

---

[1]'It is a test (a positive test, I do not assert that it is always valid negatively), that genuine
poetry can communicate before it is understood.'—T. S. Eliot, *Dante,* p. 16. /112/

it would lose if the notes could be suppressed and forgotten, yet the more important criticism might be said to be, not that it depends upon them too much, but rather that without them, and without the support of *From Ritual to Romance,* it would not lose more. It has, that is, certain limitations in any case; limitations inherent in the conditions that produced it. Comprehensiveness, in the very nature of the undertaking, must be in some sense at the cost of structure: absence of direction, of organizing principle, in life could hardly be made to subserve the highest kind of organization in art.

But when all qualifications have been urged, *The Waste Land* remains a great positive achievement, and one of the first importance for English poetry. In it a mind fully alive in the age compels a poetic triumph out of the peculiar difficulties facing a poet in the age. And in solving his own problem as a poet Mr. Eliot did more than solve the problem for himself. Even if *The Waste Land* had been, as used to be said, a 'dead end' for him, it would still have been a new start for English poetry.

But, of course, to judge it a 'dead end' was shallow. It was to ignore the implications of the effort that alone could have availed to express formlessness itself as form. So complete and vigorous a statement of the Waste Land could /113/ hardly (to risk being both crude and impertinent) forecast an exhausted, hopeless sojourn there. As for the nature of the effort, the intimacy with Dante that the poem betrays has its significance. There is no great distance in time and no gulf of any kind between the poet of *The Waste Land* and the critic who associates[1] himself later with 'a tendency — discernible even in art — toward a higher and clearer conception of Reason, and a more severe and serene control of the emotions by Reason'; and who writes[2] of Proust 'as a point of demarcation between a generation for whom the dissolution of value had in itself a positive value, and the generation which is beginning to turn its attention to an athleticism, a *training,* of the soul as severe and ascetic as the training of the body of a runner.' /114/

[1]*Criterion,* Jan. 1926, vol. iv., p. 5. /114/
[2]*Ibid.,* Oct. 1926, vol. iv., pp. 752-3. /114/

Eliot's reminiscences point to "the similarity that often lies beneath contrasting appearances, and can thus stress the essential equivalence of seemingly different experiences."

F. O. Matthiessen

THE SYSTEM OF ALLUSION

After such knowledge, what forgiveness?

In such a passage as the conclusion of 'The Burial of the Dead' Eliot reveals the way in which he himself possesses 'a sense of his own age', that 'peculiar Honesty, which, in a world too frightened to be honest, is peculiarly terrifying. It is an honesty against which the whole world conspires because it is unpleasant.' Eliot used those words in describing Blake, and a further extension of the passage is likewise relevant to his own aims in 'The Waste Land' (which he was to publish two years after this essay): 'Nothing that can be called morbid or abnormal or perverse, none of the things which exemplify the sickness of an epoch or a fashion, have this quality; only those things which, by some extraordinary labour of simplification, exhibit the essential sickness or strength of the human soul.'

In Eliot's earlier work, in such a poem as 'Sweeney among the Nightingales', or, more particularly, 'A Cooking Egg', it at first looked as though he was so absorbed in the splendours of the past that he was capable of expressing only the violent contrast between its remembered beauty and the actual dreary ugliness of contemporary existence, that he was merely prolonging one mood inherited from Flaubert of viewing human life crushed into something mean

From *The Achievement of T. S. Eliot* by F. O. Matthiessen (Boston: Houghton Mifflin and Company, 1935), Chapter II, "The Problem of the Contemporary Artist," pp. 33-44, with notes, pp. 45-54. Copyright 1935 by Oxford University Press and reprinted with their permission.

and sordid by bourgeois 'civilization'. But on closer examination it appears that his contrasts are not so clear-cut, that he is not confining himself to voicing anything so essentially limited and shallow as the inferiority of the present to the past. He /33/ is simply keenly aware of our contemporary historical consciousness, and of the problems which it creates. The modern educated man possesses a knowledge of the past to a degree hardly glimpsed a century ago, not only of one segment of the past, but, increasingly, of all pasts. If he is sensitive to what he knows, he will realize that not only does he therefore have a feeling, in Eliot's words, 'that the whole of the literature of Europe from Homer . . . has a simultaneous existence', but that also, owing to the self-consciousness which results from so much knowledge (scientific and psychological as well as historical and literary), he can have a sense in any given moment, as Eliot has remarked of Joyce, 'of everything happening at once'.

Such a realization can lead either to chaos or to a sense of the potential unity of life. The difficulty with our knowledge to-day consists in the fact that instead of giving the individual's mind release and freedom, the piling up of so many disparate and seemingly unrelated details can merely oppress him with their bewildering variety, with 'being too conscious and conscious of too much',[1] with the futility of any certainty, or, as Eliot has reflected, with the feeling that 'everybody is conscious of every question, and no one knows any answers'. The problem for the artist is to discover some unified pattern in this variety; and yet, if he believes as Eliot does that poetry should embody a man's reaction to his whole experience, also to present the full sense of its complexity. He can accomplish this double task of accurately recording what he has felt and perceived, and at the same time interpreting it, only if he grasps the similarity that often lies beneath contrasting appearances, and can thus stress the essential equivalence of seemingly different experiences. Such understanding and resultant stress form the heart of Eliot's reason for introducing so many reminiscences of other poets into the texture of his own verse. In this way he can at once suggest the extensive consciousness of the past that is inevitably possessed /34/ by any cultivated reader of to-day, and, more importantly, can greatly increase the implications of his lines by this tacit revelation of the sameness (as well as the contrasts) between the life of the present and that of other ages.[2]

Moreover, such stress is the essence of the method of 'The Waste

---

[1]The notes for this essay are printed at the end of the article—*Editor's note.*

Land', whose city, as we have seen, is many cities, or rather certain qualities resulting from the pervasive state of mind bred by mass civilization. But the structure of the poem embraces more than that. In his desire to make available for poetry the multiplicity of the modern world in the only way that the artist can, by giving it order and form, Eliot had discovered a clue in anthropology, in its exploration of ancient myths. It was not accidental or owing to any idiosyncrasy that he was affected profoundly by his reading of such a work as 'The Golden Bough', since the investigations of anthropology along with those of psychology have produced the most fundamental revolutions in contemporary thought and belief. It is noteworthy that Jessie Weston's 'From Ritual to Romance' appeared in 1920, at the very time when Eliot was seeking a coherent shape for the mass of intricate material that enters into his poem. For reading that book gave to his mind the very fillip which it needed in order to crystallize.[3] What he learned especially from it was the recurring pattern of similarity in various myths, the basic resemblance, for example, between the vegetation myths of the rebirth of the year, the fertility myths of the rebirth of the potency of man, the Christian story of the Resurrection, and the Grail legend of purification. The common source of all these myths lay in the fundamental rhythm of nature – that of the death and rebirth of the year; and their varying symbolism was an effort to explain the origin of life. Such knowledge, along with the researches of psychology, pointed to the close union in all these myths of the physical and spiritual, to the fact that their symbolism was basically sexual – in the Cup and Lance of the Grail legend as well as in the Orpheus cults; pointed, in /35/ brief, to the fundamental relation between the wellsprings of sex and religion.

The consequence of so much knowledge furnishes a condensed example of the general problem of the modern consciousness outlined above. When the investigations of anthropology reveal that surface differences between the customs and beliefs of mankind tend to mask profound resemblances, the result is both a freeing and a destruction. Taboos are removed, but sanctions wither. The purity of the Grail legend seems lost in symbols of generative significance; and yet at the same time it takes on a rich depth of primitive force that was wholly lost by Tennyson's denatured picture-book version. In such a perception of the nature of myths, of 'a common principle underlying all manifestations of life',[4] Eliot found a scaffold for his poem, a background of reference that made possible something in the nature of a musical organization. He found the specific clue to the dramatic shaping of his material when he read in Miss Weston of the frequent representation of the mystery of death and rebirth by the story of a kingdom where, the forces of the ruler having been weakened or destroyed by sickness, old age, or the ravages of war, 'the land becomes Waste, and the task of the hero is that of restoration',[5] not by pursuing advantages for himself, but by giving himself to the quest of seeking the health and salvation of the land.

The poem thus embodies simultaneously several different planes of experience, for it suggests the likenesses between various waste lands. Its quest for salvation in contemporary London is given greater volume and urgency by the additional presence of the haunted realm of medieval legend. The name of the battle where Stetson fought is that of one in which the Carthaginians were defeated, pointing the essential sameness of all wars. The opening of the final section in particular furnishes an example of the way Eliot is portraying the /36/ equivalence of different experiences by linking together various myths:

> *After the torchlight red on sweaty faces*
> *After the frosty silence in the gardens*
> *After the agony in stony places*
> *The shouting and the crying*
> *Prison and palace and reverberation*
> *Of thunder of spring over distant mountains*
> *He who was living is now dead*
> *We who were living are now dying*
> *With a little patience.*

Reminiscence here is not only of the final scenes in the life of Christ and of the gnawing bafflement of his disciples before his appearance at Emmaus. The vigil of silence and the agony of spiritual struggle are not limited to one garden; they belong to the perilous quest of Parsival or Galahad as well. The 'shouting and the crying' re-echo not only from the mob that thronged Jerusalem at the time of the Crucifixion, but also, as is made clearer in ensuing lines, from the 'hordes swarming over endless plains' in revolt in contemporary Russia. In the 'thunder of spring over distant mountains' there is likewise a hint of the vegetation myths, of the approaching rebirth of the parched dead land through the life-giving rain. Thus he who 'is now dead' is not Christ alone, but the slain Vegetation God; he is Adonis and Osiris and Orpheus.[6] And with the line, 'We who were living are now dying', the link is made back to the realm of death in life of the opening section, the realm which focuses all the elements of the poem and resounds through all its lines, the waste land of contemporary existence, likewise waiting for salvation, salvation that can come only through sacrifice, as is revealed in the final apocalyptic command reverberating through 'What the Thunder Said': 'Give, Sympathize, Control.' /37/

As a result of this method of compressing into a single moment both the memory and the sameness of other moments, it becomes apparent that in 'The Fire Sermon', the section of the poem which deals in particular with the present and the past of London, no sharply separating contrast is made between them. Squalor pollutes the modern river as it did not in Spenser's 'Prothalamion'; but there are also glimpses of beauty where

> *The river sweats*
> *Oil and tar*
> *The barges drift*
> *With the turning tide*
> *Red sails*
> *Wide*
> *To leeward, swing on the heavy spar.*

And, conversely, although mention of Elizabeth and Leicester brings an illusion of glamour, closer thought reveals that the stale pretence of their relationship left it quite as essentially empty as that between the typist and the clerk.

Use of such widely divergent details in a single poem indicates the special problem of the contemporary artist. Faced with so great a range of knowledge as a part of the modern consciousness, he can bring it to satisfactory expression in one of two ways, either by expansion or compression. It can hardly be simply a coincidence that each of these ways was carried to its full development at almost the same time, in the years directly following the War. Joyce chose the first alternative for 'Ulysses' and devoted more than a quarter of a million words to revealing the complexity involved in the passage of a single ordinary day. In the following year Eliot concentrated an interpretation of a whole condition of society into slightly over four hundred lines. That Eliot was aware of similarities in their aims is revealed in a brief essay which he published during the year after the appearance of 'The /38/ Waste Land' on 'Ulysses,

Order, and Myth'.[7] He recognized how important it had been for Joyce to find a scaffold for his work in the structure of the 'Odyssey' when he remarked that:

'In using the myth, in manipulating a continuous parallel between contemporaneity and antiquity, Mr. Joyce is pursuing a method which others must pursue after him. They will not be imitators, any more than the scientist who uses the discoveries of an Einstein in pursuing his own, independent, further investigations. It is simply a way of controlling, of ordering, of giving a shape and a significance to the immense panorama of futility and anarchy which is contemporary history. It is a method already adumbrated by Mr. Yeats, and of the need for which I believe Mr. Yeats to have been the first contemporary to be conscious.'

The utilization of such a discovery would clearly differ for the novelist and the poet. With the example of the nineteenth century behind him, Eliot naturally felt that, if the long poem was to continue to exist, there must be more to distinguish it than simply length, that its energy must be increased by the elimination of everything superfluous. To convey in poetry the feeling of the actual passage of life, to bring to expression the varied range and volume of awareness which exists in a full moment of consciousness, demanded, in Eliot's view, the strictest condensation. Above all, the impression of a fully packed content should not be weakened through the relaxed connectives of the usual narrative structure. Whatever may have been right at the time of the composition of 'The Ring and The Book', it was apparent to Eliot that to-day 'anything that can be said as well in prose can be said better in prose'. Poetry alone, through its resources of rhythm and sound, can articulate the concentrated essence of experience, and thus come closest to the universal and permanent; but it can do so only through the mastery of a concentrated form. Though he approaches the question with a much broader understanding of all the factors involved than was possessed by the author of /39/ 'The Poetic Principle', Eliot is at one with Poe in his insistence on the necessary economy of a work of art, in his belief that a poem should be constructed deliberately with the aim of producing a unified effect. Consequently, after composing the first draft of 'The Waste Land', his revisions shortened it to less than two-thirds of its original length, in order that he might best create a dramatic structure that would possess at the same time a lyrical intensity.

That Eliot does not hold up such a method of construction as an ideal necessarily to be followed is revealed from an extended comment at the very close of 'The Use of Poetry':

'To return to the question of obscurity: when all exceptions have been made, and after admitting the possible existence of minor "difficult" poets whose public must always be small, I believe that the poet naturally prefers to write for as large and miscellaneous an audience as possible, and that it is the half-educated and ill-educated, rather than the uneducated, who stand in his way: I myself should like an audience which could neither read or write. The most useful poetry, socially, would be one which could cut across all the present stratifications of public taste—stratifications which are perhaps a sign of social disintegration. The ideal medium for poetry, to my mind, and the most direct means of social "usefulness" for poetry, is the theatre. In a play of Shakespeare you get several levels of significance. For the simplest auditors there is the plot, for the more thoughtful the character and conflict of character, for the more literary the words and phrasing, for the more musically sensitive the rhythm, and for auditors of greater sensitiveness and understanding a meaning which reveals itself gradually. And I do not believe that the classification of audience is so clear-cut as this; but rather that the sensitiveness of every auditor is acted upon by all these elements at once, though in different degrees of consciousness.'

This is the kind of passage which tantalizes and infuriates pragmatic critics of the sort who believe that a good author should simply decide what he wants to do and should then go ahead and do it. They would declare such reflections either /40/ to be disingenuous or to damn out of hand the validity of Eliot's own work. But one of the fundamental secrets of art as of life is that the mature artist finds his strength partly by coming to recognize and reckon with his limitations. Just as an individual starts by accepting certain technical conventions of a given art as a means of facilitating his search for a form that will enable him to embody what he wants to express, so, as he grows in the practice of that art and as he comes to closer grips with his own character, he will know that there are only certain things that he is best fitted to do, and that he can do those adequately only through selection and long perseverance.

Eliot's extreme degree of awareness of the boundaries of his own work is very similar to Hawthorne's detached perception of the contrast between the bustling everyday Salem which surrounded him, and the realm of dim lights and dark shadows which he was meanwhile creating in 'The Scarlet Letter'. Eliot's preference for a very different kind of poetry from that which he is capable of writing likewise recalls Hawthorne's repeated statement that the kind of novels he really liked were not his own tenuous explorations of the soul, but the solid beef-and-ale stories of Trollope. This unusual degree of detachment which reverberates with loneliness, but which brings with it in compensation a special development of spiritual understanding, has grown organically out of the conditions of American life, from the isolation of the individual from the centre of European culture. Kindred isolation enabled Thoreau and Emily Dickinson to study themselves with such rare mastery. It has also enabled Poe and Henry James and Eliot, all of them possessing the excessive provincial consciousness of elements in literary tradition which Europeans would have taken for granted — and ignored — by that very consciousness to lead their European contemporaries into a more penetrating comprehension of the nature of art. /41/

Except for the two scenes of the unfinished 'Sweeney Agonistes', and his recent Book of Words for the Church pageant, 'The Rock', neither of which can finally be considered as more than a revealing experiment with form, Eliot knows that his own work is very unlike a play by Shakespeare in the levels of its appeal. Such poems as 'The Waste Land' and 'Ash Wednesday', richly significant as they are on all the higher levels which Eliot lists, virtually ignore the level of the pit altogether. But the fact remains that the sincere artist writes not the way he would, but the way he must. And the most important value of the artist to society, and the one element that lends his work enduring significance, is to give expression to the most pervading qualities of life *as he has actually known it*. That Landor and Donne have appealed to restricted audiences defines but does not destroy their excellence. And no one would think of quarrelling with Lucretius or Pascal for not reaching a 'popular' level.

If, in severest analysis, the kind of poetry Eliot is writing gives evidence of social disintegration, he has expressed that fact precisely as the poet should, not by rhetorical proclamation, but by the very feeling of contemporary life which he has presented to the sensitive reader of his lines. And he has presented this not merely as something which the reader is to know through his mind, but is to know primarily as an actual physical experience, as a part of his whole being, through the humming pulsating evidence of his senses.

But when a poet is as conscious of his aims and effects as Eliot has revealed himself to be in his remarks on 'Ulysses' as well as in the long passage from 'The Use of Poetry', there is always the suspicion lingering in the minds of some readers that his way of giving order to the content of his work is too intellectually controlled and manipulated, that what he says cannot be wholly sincere because it is not sufficiently spontaneous. It may be that the large task which Eliot set himself in 'The Waste Land' 'of giving a shape and a significance to the /42/ immense panorama of futility and anarchy' of contemporary history, caused some of the experiments which he adopted to gain that end to appear too deliberate. Certainly some of his analogies with musical structure, in particular the summation of the themes in the broken ending of the final part, have always seemed to me somewhat forced and over-theoretical. But this is very different from saying that he is a too conscious artist. Indeed, such a charge would overlook the fact that some of the poetry of the past which across the remove of time seems most 'spontaneous', that of Chaucer, for example, was actually a product of long experimentation in poetic theory fully as calculated as Eliot's. The greatest narrative poem in the language, 'Troilus and Criseyde', beats with equally genuine emotion in the passages where Chaucer is translating Boccaccio directly as in those where he is manipulating the structure of the Italian's poem to suit his own ends.

Despite some of the protests of the nineteenth century on behalf of the untutored genius, it still appears that the more conscious the artist the better, if that consciousness implies the degree of fullness to which he has mastered the unending subtleties of his craft. But I have mentioned Chaucer also to point a difference in modern art. As my paragraphs on our highly developed historical sense tried to indicate, Eliot as a poet is not only inevitably acquainted with a great range of possible techniques, as all expert poets since the Renaissance have increasingly been; he is, in addition, highly aware of the processes of the mind itself. That particular kind of consciousness is in part what led him to feel the necessity of grounding the structure of his longest poem in something outside himself, in an objective pattern of myths.

"Ulysses', to be sure, furnishes an even fuller example of how a contemporary artist has mastered the problem of consciousness in a similar way. When one contemplates the overwhelming elaborateness of Joyce's construction, the almost unbelievable degree to which he has worked out the parallel /43/ of even the smallest details in his narrative with those in the 'Odyssey' (to say nothing of his intricate scheme of correspondences between the sections of his work and various colours, arts, bodily organs, &c.), one begins by wondering why his huge creative power has not been stultified by this fantastic heaping up of seemingly pointless erudition, of practically none of which is it necessary for the reader to be aware in order to follow with full understanding the progress of Bloom's and Stephen's day. But finally one realizes that the very *completeness* of this arbitrary external structure may have been the one thing that gave to Joyce's scholastic mind, deprived of faith but still possessing the ingrained habits of logical formal thought, the greatest creative release possible to him, by providing him with an entire scaffold — and one which has the advantage of being one of the best stories in Western civilization — on which to build his work.

And in case there should be some feeling that either Joyce or Eliot has revealed a kind of bookish weakness in turning for his structure to literature rather than to life, it should be recollected that Shakespeare himself created hardly any of his plots, and that by the very fact of taking ready-made the pattern of his characters' actions, he was able to devote his full attention to endowing them with life. It is only an uninformed prejudice which holds that literature must start from actual personal experience. It certainly must end with giving a full sense of life; but it is not at all necessary that the poet should have undergone in his own person what he describes. Indeed, the more catholic the range of the artist, the more obviously impossible that would be. The poet's imagination can work equally well on his reading as on the raw material of his senses. In fact, it is a mark of full human maturity, as Eliot has revealed in his discussion of the metaphysical poets, that there should not be a separation in an individual's sensibility between reading and experience any more than between emotion and thought.[8] /44/

NOTES

1. F. R. Leavis, 'New Bearings in English Poetry' (London, 1932), uses a similar phrase on p. 94. Mr. Leavis's interpretation of Eliot, though acutely perceptive of certain details to which I have been indebted particularly in this chapter, suffers from a certain over-intensity. He seems to be writing continually on the defensive as though he were the apostle of modern art to an unappreciative world. As a result his criticism, though eager, is somewhat wanting in balance and perspective.

2. This matter of Eliot's use of his reading (a hint of which he picked up from the symbolists, but which he has carried to far greater lengths) has been a stumbling-block to so many readers of his poetry that it requires further comment. On the one hand are those who believe that it is impossible to understand him without possessing the ability to recognize all his varied allusions, and who, therefore, indifferent to the seemingly hopeless and unrewarding task of tracing down both the wide and specialized range of his particular equipment of knowledge, have given him up as 'a poet for the learned'. On the other hand are the smaller body of readers who have done the greatest disservice to his reputation—I mean those who regard his poetry as a kind of hidden mystery for the cognoscenti. They cast the snob-vote for him. 'What?' they ask, 'you haven't read 'The Golden Bough'? You don't own a Tarot pack? You haven't studied the Upanishads? You didn't even recognize that allusion to Verlaine? Why, my dear, how can you expect to understand Mr. Eliot?'

The shortest answer (which, I hope, is given full confirmation during the course of my essay) is that you begin to understand Eliot precisely as you begin to understand any other poet: by listening to the lines, by regarding their pattern as a self-enclosed whole, by listening to what is being communicated instead of looking for something that isn't. On the particular matter of what is accomplished by Eliot's literary allusions, and what equipment is necessary to comprehend them, consider the opening passage of 'The Fire Sermon':

> The river's tent is broken: the last fingers of leaf
> Clutch and sink into the wet bank. The wind /45/
> Crosses the brown land, unheard. The nymphs are departed.
> Sweet Thames, run softly, till I end my song.
> The river bears no empty bottles, sandwich papers,
> Silk handkerchiefs, cardboard boxes, cigarette ends
> Or other testimony of summer nights. The nymphs are
>   departed.
> And their friends, the loitering heirs of city directors;
> Departed, have left no addresses.
> By the waters of Leman I sat down and wept . . . .
> Sweet Thames, run softly till I end my song,
> Sweet Thames, run softly, for I speak not loud or long.
> But at my back in a cold blast I hear
> The rattle of the bones, and chuckle spread from ear to ear.

If one reads these lines with an attentive ear and is sensitive to their sudden shifts in movement, the contrast between the actual Thames and the idealized vision of it during an age before it flowed through a megalopolis is sharply conveyed by that movement itself, whether or not one recognizes the refrain to be from Spenser. If one does have the lovely pictures of his 'Prothalamion' in mind, there is then added to the contrast a fuller volume and poignancy. In like manner with the startling quickening of pace in the final two lines and the terrifying shudder they induce: it is not necessary to refer this effect to Marvell's 'Coy Mistress', although if the effect of the sudden electric shift in cadence in that poem is also in the reader's ear, there is again a heightening.

In neither of these cases is anything demanded of the reader different in kind from what is demanded by Milton's 'Lycidas'. A single careful reading of that poem can fascinate the reader with its extraordinary melodic richness and make him want to press on to a full comprehension of its intricate form, of the way its structure builds up through a series of climaxes. But this can be understood only through some knowledge of the whole elaborate convention that Milton inherited from the classical and Renaissance pastoral. In particular, there are many passages, the fullest relish of which depends upon the reader's bringing with him the memory of the way a similar situation has been handled by Virgil and Theocritus. In addition, certain well-known lines /46/ require for the grasp of their sense at least as full literary annotation as any passage in Eliot. For instance,

> Next Camus, reverend sire, went footing slow,
> His mantle hairy, and his bonnet sedge,
> Inwrought with figures dim, and on the edge
> Like to that sanguine flower inscribed with woe.

The wealth of mythology compressed into those lines would require a long paragraph if it were to be elucidated in prose.

The point with any poem is that if the reader starts by being enchanted by the movement of the lines, then gradually his mind furnishes itself with the information necessary to understand what they are telling him. In the case of the modern reader of a poem in a Renaissance tradition, this means reminding himself of certain mythological details once common property among educated readers, but now increasingly forgotten. In the case of reading a contemporary poet, it is more a question of accustoming yourself to an unfamiliar procedure that breaks through your preconceptions of what poetry should be (precisely as Wordsworth broke through preconceptions inherited from the eighteenth century). As Eliot remarked in the Conclusion to 'The Use of Poetry':

'The uses of poetry certainly vary as society alters, as the public to be addressed changes. . . . The difficulty of poetry (and modern poetry is supposed to be difficult) . . . may be due just to novelty: we know the ridicule accorded in turn to Wordsworth, Shelley and Keats, Tennyson and Browning—but must remark that Browning was the first to be *called* difficult; hostile critics of the earlier poets found them difficult, but called them silly. Or difficulty may be caused by the reader's having been told, or having suggested to himself, that the poem is going to prove difficult. The ordinary reader, when warned against the obscurity of a poem, is apt to be thrown into a state of consternation very unfavourable to poetic receptivity. Instead of beginning, as he should, in a state of sensitivity, he obfuscates his senses by the desire to be clever and to look very hard for something, he doesn't know what—or else by the desire not to be taken in. There is such a thing as stage fright, but what such readers have is pit or gallery fright. The more seasoned reader, he who has reached, in these matters, a state of greater *purity,* does not bother about understanding; /47/ not, at least, at first. I know that some of the poetry to which I am most devoted is poetry which I did not understand at first reading; some is poetry which I am not sure I understand yet: for instance, Shakespeare's. And finally, there is the difficulty caused by the author's having left out something which the reader is used to finding; so that the reader, bewildered, gropes about for what is absent, and puzzles his head for a kind of "meaning" which is not there, and is not meant to be there.'

It is also relevant to note how this passage from 'The Fire Sermon' furnishes an example of Eliot's way of suggesting sameness at the heart of contrast. 'The nymphs are departed': the first use of that statement, followed as it is by the line from Spenser, serves to build up the pastoral atmosphere: 'The river nymphs are departed with the oncoming of winter.' But as the ensuing lines present the picture of the present Thames in summer, the statement takes on another meaning: 'The age of romantic loveliness is gone.'

Then, when the statement is repeated a few lines later, the nymphs themselves have altered; they have now become decidedly flesh and blood. But the feeling expressed is not that the past was wholly noble and the present base. Instead, it is being suggested, if only in a minor undertone, that this glimpse of present life along the river, depressingly sordid as it is, being human cannot be wholly different from human life in the past. And, concurrently, the idealized Elizabethan young men and women who appear as attendants in Spenser's marriage songs begin to be seen with new eyes. They cannot be wholly unlike the present idle young men about town and their nymphs; and this touch of humanity removes them from the realm of the abstract and endows them with actuality. In such a manner the undertones of this 'resembling contrast' have grown directly from the depth of Eliot's psychological perception into the nature of life, of the way, for example, in which nobility and baseness are inextricably mingled in even the finest individual.

3. A point necessary to mention is that an appreciation of Eliot's poem is not dependent upon reading Miss Weston's study. I had been enjoying 'The Waste Land' for several years before an /48/ interest in exploring the effect of Eliot's reading upon his development brought me to 'From Ritual to Romance'. As a result of having read that book I can now follow more distinctly the logical steps by which Eliot was led to compose his structure, and can also perceive in detail the kind of stimulus and release that the book gave to his mind. I am also enabled to understand more fully how some of the widely disparate details fall into the completed pattern. For example, I had previously taken the presence of the 'wicked pack of cards' in the opening section to be simply a sharp dramatic device by which Eliot introduced his characters and at the same time stressed the point of their shifting identity: that, observed under varying and contrasting appearances, human beings remain essentially the same throughout different ages. I have never seen a Tarot pack (and, if I had to bet, my money would say that neither had Eliot himself). But Miss Weston mentions that its four suits are Cup, Lance, Sword, and Dish, which thus correspond to the sexual symbolism of the Grail; and that the original use of these cards was 'not to foretell the Future in general, but to predict the rise and fall of the waters which brought fertility to the land' (p. 76). Through such knowledge the exact emotional relevance to the poem of this 'wicked pack' is obviously brought into new focus.

But with the exception of a few such illuminating details, I question whether Miss Weston's valuable study has enabled me to feel the poem more intensely. For nearly everything of importance from her book that is apposite to an appreciation of 'The Waste Land', particularly her central emphasis on the analogous ways by which various myths express the mysteries of sex and religion, has been incorporated into the structure of the poem itself, or into Eliot's Notes. Unlike many sections of Pound's 'Cantos', 'The Waste Land' does not require recourse to the poet's reading in order to become comprehensible. Its structure is pre-eminently self-contained.

The very presence of the Notes may seem to give a denial to that assertion. They are certainly an extremely artificial device, though not without precedent in English poetry, as 'The Shepherds' Calendar' could illustrate. But Spenser's desire there to have his poems rival the works of classical antiquity even to their /49/ appearance in a volume with annotations by the anonymous E. K. (who was most probably Spenser himself or at least a close collaborator), does not play any part in Eliot's intention. His Notes are simply a consequence of his desire to strip the form of his poem to its barest essentials in order to secure his concentrated effect. Such elimination, particularly when added to his method of using his reading as an integral part of his experience, demanded certain signposts of elucidation if the reader was to follow the exact course. And, as I have already indicated in my discussion of the closing lines of 'The Burial of the Dead', it is obviously necessary, for *full* understanding of some of his passages, to be aware of the special context of his allusions to other poets. In all cases when Eliot thinks that context essential to the reader of 'The Waste Land' he has given the reference, as in this instance to the 'Inferno', 'The White Devil', and 'Les Fleurs du Mal'. In the case of some of his less familiar allusions where the actual phrasing of the original constitutes part of his effect, he has also quoted the relevant passage. For example:

> *But at my back from time to time I hear*
> *The sound of horns and motors, which shall bring*
> *Sweeney to Mrs. Porter in the spring.*

These lines, by themselves, without the need of any reference, etch a sharp description of the surroundings of 'the dull canal . . . round behind the gashouse'. Most present-day readers of poetry would be able to supply the surprising contrast:

> *But at my back I always hear*
> *Time's wingèd chariot hurrying near,*

so that Eliot simply mentions 'To His Coy Mistress' in a note. But to enable the reader also to hear this 'sound of horns' in a double way, it is necessary for Eliot to add the lines from the little-known Elizabethan poet, John Day:

When of the sudden, listening, you shall hear
A noise of horns and hunting, which shall bring
Actaeon to Diana in the spring,
Where all shall see her naked skin. . . . /50/

And no matter how much one may object to the existence of the Notes in general, it would be hard to deny the flash of tightly packed wit that is struck by the incongruous contrast between the 'naked skin' of Diana and that of Mrs. Porter.

Some of the more general references in the Notes help to sharpen the definition of the outlines of Eliot's structure. The self-consuming burning of sterile passion which is the theme of 'The Fire Sermon' receives added emphasis from the pertinent reminder of the exact expression of that theme by Buddha and St. Augustine, though no reading of their work is required for understanding the poem. I have not yet read the Upanishad from which Eliot borrowed the onomatopoeic representation of 'what the thunder said'; but it is perfectly clear from his own lines what an excellent 'objective correlative' he found in that legend.

My own chief objection to the Notes is the occasional tone of what Eliot himself, in relation to passages in 'The Sacred Wood', described as 'pontifical solemnity'. But that impression should be qualified by the admission that some of the notes which struck me at first as useless pedantry or deliberate mystification of the reader, particularly the one on Tiresias, I now recognize as very useful to the interpretation of the poem. The objection to stiffness in phrasing still remains, but this quality was perhaps due in part to Eliot's desire to state the necessary details as briefly as he could; and owing to the largeness of his undertaking in this poem and the inevitable limitations of his own temperament, this was possibly the price he had to pay in order to avoid what he would have considered muffling the energy of his poem by extended connecting links in the text itself.

The stiffness may also be due to Eliot's shyness at speaking in his own person, a quality which has likewise taken itself out in the occasional ponderous over-and under-statements in his Prefaces, and in his 'Criterion' Commentaries. In these Notes it crops up in a curious double-edged irony, where he appears to be mocking himself for writing the note at the same time that he wants to convey something by it. Certainly the note on the hermit-thrush which tells us that it is *turdus aonalaschkae pallasii* and quotes a description from Chapman's 'Handbook of Birds of Eastern North America', would seem as though it were the /51/ desperate effort of J. Alfred Prufrock himself to say something important, but ending only in irrelevance. But actually the note ends with a telling sentence: 'Its "water-dripping song" is justly celebrated.' And by that sentence Eliot has given a precise suggestion of the very sound from which his lines took rise (as remarked at the close of my chapter on the auditory imagination); and for ornithologists even the passage from Chapman would have the advantage of exact description.

Comparable to Eliot's use of Notes in 'The Waste Land' is the frequent presence, throughout his work, of epigraphs for individual poems – though this device is not at all open to the objection of not being sufficiently structural. Again the intention is to enable the poet to secure a condensed expression in the poem itself, as well as to induce the reader to realize, even from the moment before the poem begins, that in reading poetry every word should be paid full attention. In each case the epigraph is designed to form an integral part of the effect of the poem; and in the most successful instances a subtle aura of association is added. 'Mistah Kurtz – he dead' – the harrowing climax of Conrad's 'Heart of Darkness', his full expression of utter horror, epitomizes in a sentence the very tone of blasphemous hopelessness which issues from 'The Hollow Men'. And certainly the closed circle of Prufrock's frightened isolation is sharply underlined by inscribing this speech from the 'Inferno': 'If I thought my answer were to one who ever could return to the world, this flame should shake no more; but since, if what I hear be true, none ever did return alive from this depth, without fear of infamy I answer thee.' Prufrock can give utterance in soliloquy to his debate with himself only because he knows that no one will overhear him. The point of calling this poem a 'Love Song' lies in the irony that it will never be sung; that Prufrock will never dare to voice what he feels.

And as a final detail to this note on Notes, it is worth observing that Eliot uses his titles as well as his epigraphs as integral elements in his effect, to reiterate his belief that in writing poetry every word on the page should be designed to count. Often, in the earlier poems, the aim of the title was to surprise the reader out of all complacency. Thus 'Sweeney among the Nightingales', /52/ which is in itself a condensed metaphysical conceit; thus also the double meaning of 'Sweeney Erect'. 'Burbank with a Baedeker: Bleistein with a Cigar' dramatically sets a stage; but in this case the ensuing epigraph which is largely composed of phrases from other writers referring to events in Venice – for example, from 'Othello', 'The

Aspern Papers', and Browning's 'A Toccata of Galuppi's', though calculated to call up the reader's usual wide range of associations with that city, is too much of a pastiche to be very effective. And lastly, the startling 'A Cooking Egg' requires for its comprehension the occult knowledge that an egg which is no longer fresh enough to be eaten by itself, but must be used in cooking, is so described with the accent on the participle. Thus the title relates to the epigraph from Villon, which also tells the age and condition of the hero of the poem:

En l'an trentiesme de mon aage
Que toutes més hontes j'ay beues. . . .

4. Weston, p. 36.

5. Ibid., p. 21.

6. This point was noted by Hugh Ross Williamson, 'The Poetry of T. S. Eliot' (London, 1933), p. 135. Mr. Williamson's book, though not particularly mature in its critical observations, is a useful manual containing a good deal of relevant explanation, to which I have been frequently indebted.

7. 'The Dial', November 1923, pp. 480-3.

8. Since writing this paragraph I have re-read the passage in Henry James's essay 'The Art of Fiction' which expresses so exactly the relation between literature and experience which I have attempted to elucidate that I reproduce it here. In addition, it indicates once again a fundamental sameness in point of view between James and Eliot. James's rejoinder to the statement that 'the novelist must write from experience' runs as follows:

'It is equally excellent and inconclusive to say that one must write from experience. . . . What kind of experience is intended, and where does it begin and end? Experience is never limited, and it is never /53/ complete; it is an immense sensibility, a kind of huge spiderweb, of the finest silken threads, suspended in the chamber of consciousness and catching every air-borne particle in its tissue. It is the very atmosphere of the mind; and when the mind is imaginative — much more when it happens to be that of a man of genius — it takes to itself the faintest hints of life, it converts the very pulses of the air into revelations. The young lady living in a village has only to be a damsel upon whom nothing is lost to make it quite unfair (as it seems to me) to declare to her that she shall have nothing to say about the military. Greater miracles have been seen than that, imagination assisting, she should speak the truth about some of these gentlemen. I remember an English novelist, a woman of genius, telling me that she was much commended for the impression she had managed to give in one of her tales of the nature and way of life of the French Protestant youth. She had been asked where she learned so much about this recondite being, she had been congratulated on her peculiar opportunities. These opportunities consisted in her having once, in Paris, as she ascended a staircase, passed an open door where, in the household of a *pasteur,* some of the young Protestants were seated at table round a finished meal. The glimpse made a picture; it lasted only a moment, but that moment was experience. She had got her impression, and she evolved her type. She knew what youth was, and what Protestantism; she also had the advantage of having seen what it was to be French; so that she converted these ideas into a concrete image and produced a reality. Above all, however, she was blessed with the faculty which when you give it an inch takes an ell, and which for the artist is a much greater source of strength than any accident of residence or of place in the social scale. The power to guess the unseen from the seen, to trace the implication of things, to judge the whole piece by the pattern, the condition of feeling life, in general, so completely that you are well on your way to knowing any particular corner of it—this cluster of gifts may almost be said to constitute experience, and they occur in country and in town, and in the most differing stages of education. If experience consists of impressions, it may be said that impressions *are* experience, just as (have we not seen it?) they are the very air we breathe. Therefore, if I should certainly say to a novice, "Write from experience, and experience only", I should feel that this was rather a tantalizing monition if I were not careful immediately to add, "Try to be one of the people on whom nothing is lost!"' /54/

"Life devoid of meaning is death; sacrifice, even the sacrificial death, may be life-giving, an awakening to life."

Cleanth Brooks

THE BELIEFS EMBODIED IN THE WORK

Though much has been written on *The Waste Land*, it will not be difficult to show that most of its critics misconceive entirely the theme and the structure of the poem. There has been little or no attempt to deal with it as a unified whole. F. R. Leavis and F. O. Matthiessen have treated large sections of the poem in detail, and I am obviously indebted to both of them. I believe, however, that Leavis makes some positive errors of interpretation. I find myself in almost complete agreement with Matthiessen in his commentary on the sections which he deals with in his *Achievement of T. S. Eliot*, but the plan of his book does not allow for a complete consecutive examination of the poem.

In view of the state of criticism with regard to the poem, it is best for us to approach it frankly on the basis of its theme. I prefer, however, not to raise just here the question of how important it is for the reader to have an explicit intellectual account of the various symbols and a logical account of their relationships. It may well be that such rationalization is no more than a scaffolding to be got out of the way before we contemplate the poem itself as poem. But many readers (including myself) find the erection of such a scaf-

From *Modern Poetry and the Tradition* by Cleanth Brooks (Chapel Hill: The University of North Carolina Press, 1939), Chapter 7, *"The Waste Land:* Critique of the Myth," pp. 136-172. Reprinted by permission of the publisher.

folding valuable—if not absolutely necessary—and if some readers will be tempted to lay more stress upon the scaffolding than they should, there are perhaps still more readers who, without the help of such a scaffolding, will be prevented from getting at the poem at all. /136/

The basic symbol used, that of the waste land, is taken of course, from Miss Jessie Weston's *From Ritual to Romance*. In the legends which she treats there, the land has been blighted by a curse. The crops do not grow and the animals cannot reproduce. The plight of the land is summed up by, and connected with, the plight of the lord of the land, the Fisher King, who has been rendered impotent by maiming or sickness. The curse can be removed only by the appearance of a knight who will ask the meanings of the various symbols which are displayed to him in the castle. The shift in meaning from physical to spiritual sterility is easily made, and was, as a matter of fact, made in certain of the legends. As Eliot has pointed out, a knowledge of this symbolism is essential for an understanding of the poem.

Of hardly less importance to the reader, however, is a knowledge of Eliot's basic method. *The Waste Land* is built on a major contrast—a device which is a favorite of Eliot's and is to be found in many of his poems, particularly his later poems. The contrast is between two kinds of life and two kinds of death. Life devoid of meaning is death; sacrifice, even the sacrificial death, may be life-giving, an awakening to life. The poem occupies itself to a great extent with this paradox, and with a number of variations upon it.

Eliot has stated the matter quite explicitly himself in one of his essays. In his "Baudelaire" he says: "One aphorism which has been especially noticed is the following: *la volupté unique et suprême de l'amour gît dans la certitude de faire le mal*. This means, I think, that Baudelaire has perceived that what distinguishes the relations of man and woman from the copulation of beasts is the knowledge of Good and Evil (of *moral* Good and Evil which are not natural Good and Bad or puritan Right and Wrong). Having an imperfect, vague romantic conception of Good, he was at least able to understand that the sexual act as evil is more dignified, less boring, than as the natural, 'life-giving,' /137/ cheery automatism of the modern world. . . . So far as we are human, what we do must be either evil or good; so far as we do evil or good, we are human; and it is better, in a paradoxical way, to do evil than to do nothing: at least, *we exist* [italics mine]." The last statement is highly important for an understanding of *The Waste Land.* The fact that men have lost the knowledge of good and evil, keeps them from being alive, and is the justification for viewing the modern waste land as a realm in which the inhabitants do not even exist.

This theme is stated in the quotation which prefaces the poem. The Sybil says: "I wish to die." Her statement has several possible interpretations. For one thing, she is saying what the people who inhabit the waste land are saying. But she may also be saying what the speaker of "The Journey of the Magi" says: ". . . this Birth was/ Hard and bitter agony for us, like Death, our death/. . . I should be glad of another death."

I

The first section of "The Burial of the Dead" develops the theme of the attractiveness of death, or of the difficulty in rousing oneself from the death in life in which the people of the waste land live. Men are afraid to live in reality. April, the month of rebirth, is not the most joyful season but the cruelest. Winter at least kept us warm in forgetful snow. The idea is one which Eliot has stressed elsewhere. Earlier in "Gerontion" he had written

> In the juvescence of the year
> Came Christ the tiger
> . . . .
> The tiger springs in the new year. Us he devours.

More lately, in *Murder in the Cathedral,* he has the chorus say /138/

> We do not wish anything to happen.
> Seven years we have lived quietly,
> Succeeded in avoiding notice,
> Living and partly living.

And in another passage: "Now I fear disturbance of the quiet seasons." Men dislike to be roused from their death-in-life.

The first part of "The Burial of the Dead" introduces this theme through a sort of a reverie on the part of the protagonist—a reverie in which speculation on life glides off into memory of an actual conversation in the Hofgarten and back into speculation again. The function of the conversation is to establish the class and character of the protagonist. The reverie is resumed with line 19.

> What are the roots that clutch, what branches grow
> Out of this stony rubbish?

The protagonist answers for himself:

> Son of man,
> You cannot say, or guess, for you know only
> A heap of broken images, where the sun beats,
> And the dead tree gives no shelter, the cricket no relief,
> And the dry stone no sound of water.

In this passage there are references to Ezekiel and to Ecclesiastes, and these references indicate what it is that men no longer know: The passage referred to in Ezekiel 2, pictures a world thoroughly secularized:

1. And he said unto me, Son of man, stand upon thy feet, and I will speak unto thee.
2. And the spirit entered into me when he spake unto me, and set me upon my feet, that I heard him that spake unto me.
3. And he said unto me, Son of man, I send thee to the children of Israel, to a rebellious nation that hath rebelled /139/ against me: they and their fathers have transgressed against me, even unto this very day.

Other passages from Ezekiel are relevant to the poem, Chapter 37 in particular, which describes Ezekiel's waste land, where the prophet, in his vision of the valley of dry bones, contemplates the "burial of the dead" and is asked: "Son of man, can these bones live? And I answered, O Lord God, thou knowest. 4. Again he said unto me, Prophesy over these bones, and say unto them, O ye dry bones, hear the word of the Lord."

One of Ezekiel's prophecies was that Jerusalem would be conquered and the people led away into the Babylonian captivity. That captivity is alluded to in Section III of *The Waste Land*, line 182, where the Thames becomes the "waters of Leman."

The passage from Ecclesiastes 12, alluded to in Eliot's notes, describes the same sort of waste land:

1. Remember now thy Creator in the days of thy youth, while the evil days come not, nor the years draw nigh, when thou shalt say, I have no pleasure in them;

2. While the sun, or the light, or the moon, or the stars, be not darkened, nor the clouds return after the rain;

3. In the day when the keepers of the house shall tremble, and the strong men shall bow themselves, and the grinders cease because they are few, and those that look out of the windows be darkened,

4. And the doors shall be shut in the streets, when the sound of the grinding is low, and he shall rise up at the voice of the bird, and all the daughters of musick shall be brought low;

5. Also when they shall be afraid of that which is high, and fears shall be in the way, and the almond tree shall flourish, and the grasshopper shall be a burden, *and desire shall fail* [italics mine]: because man goeth to his long home, and the mourners go about the streets;

6. Or ever the silver cord be loosed, or the golden bowl be broken, or the pitcher be broken at the fountain, or the wheel broken at the cistern. /140/

7. Then shall the dust return to the earth as it was: and the spirit shall return unto God who gave it.

8. Vanity of vanities, saith the preacher; all is vanity.

A reference to this passage is also evidently made in the nightmare vision of Section V of the poem.

The next section of "The Burial of the Dead" which begins with the scrap of song quoted from Wagner (perhaps another item in the reverie of the protagonist), states the opposite half of the paradox which underlies the poem: namely, that life at its highest moments of meaning and intensity resembles death. The song from Act I of Wagner's *Tristan und Isolde, "Frisch weht der Wind,"* is sung in the opera by a young sailor aboard the ship which is bringing Isolde to Cornwall. The *"Irisch kind"* of the song does not properly apply to Isolde at all. The song is merely one of happy and naïve love. It brings to the mind of the protagonist an experience of love— the vision of the hyacinth girl as she came back from the hyacinth garden. The poet says

> . . . my eyes failed, I was neither
> Living nor dead, and I knew nothing,
> Looking into the heart of light, the silence.

The line which immediately follows this passage, *"Oed' und leer das*

Meer," seems at first to be simply an extension of the last figure: that is, "Empty and wide the sea [of silence]." But the line, as a matter of fact, makes an ironic contrast; for the line, as it occurs in Act III of the opera, is the reply of the watcher who reports to the wounded Tristan that Isolde's ship is nowhere in sight; the sea is empty. And, though the *"Irisch kind"* of the first quotation is not Isolde, the reader familiar with the opera will apply it to Isolde when he comes to the line *"Oed' und leer das Meer."* For the question in the song is in essence Tristan's question in Act III: "My Irish child, where dwellest thou?" The two quotations from the opera which frame the ecstasy-of-love passage thus take on a new meaning in the altered con- /141/ text. In the first, love is happy; the boat rushes on with a fair wind behind it. In the second, love is absent; the sea is wide and empty. And the last quotation reminds us that even love cannot exist in the waste land.

The next passage, that in which Madame Sosostris figures, calls for further reference to Miss Weston's book. As Miss Weston has shown, the Tarot cards were originally used to determine the event of highest importance to the people, the rising of the waters. Madame Sosostris has fallen a long way from the high function of her predecessors. She is engaged merely in vulgar fortune-telling — is merely one item in a generally vulgar civilization. But the symbols of the Tarot pack are still unchanged. The various characters are still inscribed on the cards, and she is reading in reality (though she does not know it) the fortune of the protagonist. She finds that his card is that of the drowned Phoenician Sailor, and so she warns him against death by water, not realizing any more than do the other inhabitants of the modern waste land that the way into life may be by death itself. The drowned Phoenician Sailor is a type of the fertility god whose image was thrown into the sea annually as a symbol of the death of summer. As for the other figures in the pack: Belladonna, the Lady of the Rocks, is woman in the waste land. The man with three staves, Eliot says he associates rather arbitrarily with the Fisher King. The term "arbitrarily" indicates that we are not to attempt to find a logical connection here. (It may be interesting to point out, however, that Eliot seems to have given, in a later poem, his reason for making the association. In "The Hollow Men" he writes, speaking as one of the Hollow Men:

Let me also wear
Such deliberate disguises

Rat's coat, crowskin, crossed staves
In a field
Behaving as the wind behaves. /142/

The figure is that of a scarecrow, fit symbol of the man who possesses
no reality, and fit type of the Fisher King, the maimed, impotent
king who ruled over the waste land of the legend. The man with
three staves in the deck of cards may thus have appealed to the poet
as an appropriate figure to which to assign the function of the Fisher
King, although the process of identification was too difficult to expect the reader to follow and although knowledge of the process was
not necessary to an understanding of the poem.)

The Hanged Man, who represents the hanged god of Frazer
(including the Christ), Eliot states in a note, is associated with the
hooded figure who appears in "What the Thunder Said." That he is
hooded accounts for Madame Sosostris' inability to see him; or
rather, here again the palaver of the modern fortune-teller is turned
to new and important account by the poet's shifting the reference
into a new and serious context. The Wheel and the one-eyed merchant will be discussed later.

After the Madame Sosostris passage, Eliot proceeds to compli-
cate his symbols for the sterility and unreality of the modern waste
land by associating it with Baudelaire's *"fourmillante cité"* and
with Dante's Limbo. The passages already quoted from Eliot's essay
on Baudelaire will indicate one of the reasons why Baudelaire's
lines are evoked here. In Baudelaire's city, dream and reality seem
to mix, and it is interesting that Eliot in "The Hollow Men" refers
to this same realm of death-in-life as "death's dream kingdom"
in contradistinction to "death's other kingdom."

The references to Dante are most important. The line, "I had
not thought death had undone so many," is taken from the Third
Canto of the *Inferno*; the line, "Sighs, short and infrequent, were
exhaled," from the Fourth Canto. Mr. Matthiessen has already
pointed out that the Third Canto deals with Dante's Limbo which is
occupied by those who on earth had "lived without praise or blame."
They share this abode with the angels "who were not rebels, nor
were faithful to God, but were for themselves." They ex- /143/
emplify almost perfectly the secular attitude which dominates the
modern world. Their grief, according to Dante, arises from the fact
that they "have no hope of death; and their blind life is so debased,
that they are envious of every other lot." But though they may not
hope for death, Dante calls them "these wretches who never were

alive." The people described in the Fourth Canto are those who lived virtuously but who died before the proclamation of the Gospel — they are the unbaptized. They form the second of the two classes of people who inhabit the modern waste land: those who are secularized and those who have no knowledge of the faith. Without a faith their life is in reality a death. To repeat the sentence from Eliot previously quoted: "So far as we do evil or good, we are human; and it is better, in a paradoxical way, to do evil than to do nothing: at least, we exist."

The Dante and Baudelaire references, then, come to the same thing as the allusion to the waste land of the medieval legends; and these various allusions, drawn from widely differing sources, enrich the comment on the modern city so that it becomes "unreal" on a number of levels: as seen through "the brown fog of a winter dawn"; as the medieval waste land and Dante's Limbo and Baudelaire's Paris are unreal.

The reference to Stetson stresses again the connection between the modern London of the poem and Dante's hell. After the statement, "I could never have believed death had undone so many," follow the words, "After I had distinguished some among them, I saw and knew the shade of him who made, through cowardice, the great refusal." The protagonist, like Dante, sees among the inhabitants of the contemporary waste land one whom he recognizes. (The name "Stetson" I take to have no ulterior significance. It is merely an ordinary name such as might be borne by the friend one might see in a crowd in a great city.) Mylae, as Mr. Matthiessen has pointed out, is the name of a battle between the Romans and the Carthaginians in the Punic /144/ War. The Punic War was a trade war — might be considered a rather close parallel to our late war. At any rate, it is plain that Eliot in having the protagonist address the friend in a London street as one who was with him in the Punic War rather than as one who was with him in the World War is making the point that all the wars are one war; all experience, one experience. As Eliot put the idea in *Murder in the Cathedral*:

> We do not know very much of the future
> Except that from generation to generation
> The same things happen again and again

I am not sure that Leavis and Matthiessen are correct in inferring that the line, "That corpse you planted last year in your garden," refers to the attempt to bury a memory. But whether or not this is true, the line certainly refers also to the buried god of the old fertility rites. It also is to be linked with the earlier passage – "What are the roots that clutch, what branches grow," etc. This allusion to the buried god will account for the ironical, almost taunting tone of the passage. The burial of the dead is now a sterile planting – without hope. But the advice to "keep the Dog far hence," in spite of the tone, is, I believe, well taken and serious. The passage in Webster goes as follows

> But keep the wolf far thence, that's foe to men,
> For with his nails he'll dig them up again.

Why does Eliot turn the wolf into a dog? And why does he reverse the point of importance from the animal's normal hostility to men to its friendliness? If, as some critics have suggested, he is merely interested in making a reference to Webster's darkest play, why alter the line? I am inclined to take the Dog (the capital letter is Eliot's) as Humanitarianism* and the related philosophies which, in their /145/ concern for man, extirpate the supernatural – dig up the corpse of the buried god and thus prevent the rebirth of life. For the general idea, see Eliot's essay, "The Humanism of Irving Babbitt."

The last line of "The Burial of the Dead" – "You! hypocrite lecteur! – mon semblable, – mon frère!" the quotation from Baudelaire, completes the universalization of Stetson begun by the reference to Mylae. Stetson is every man including the reader and Mr. Eliot himself.

II

If "The Burial of the Dead" gives the general abstract statement of the situation, the second part of *The Waste Land*, "A Game of Chess," gives a more concrete illustration. The easiest contrast in this section – and one which may easily blind the casual reader to a continued emphasis on the contrast between the two kinds of life, or the two kinds of death, already commented on – is the contrast between life in a rich and magnificent setting, and life in the low and vulgar setting of a London pub. But both scenes, however antithetical they may appear superficially, are scenes

---

*The reference is perhaps more general still: it may include Naturalism, and Science in the popular conception as the new magic which will enable man to conquer his environment completely. /145/

taken from the contemporary waste land. In both of them life has lost its meaning.

I am particularly indebted to Mr. Allen Tate's comment on the first part of this section. To quote from him, "The woman . . . is, I believe, the symbol of man at the present time. He is surrounded by the grandeurs of the past, but he does not participate in them; they don't sustain him." And to quote from another section of his commentary: "The rich experience of the great tradition depicted in the room receives a violent shock in contrast with a game that symbolizes the inhuman abstraction of the modern mind." Life has no meaning; history has no meaning; there is no answer to the question: "What shall we ever do?" The only thing that has meaning is the abstract game which they are to play, a game in which the meaning is assigned /146/ and arbitrary, meaning by convention only – in short, a game of chess.

This interpretation will account in part for the pointed reference to Cleopatra in the first lines of the section. But there is, I believe, a further reason for the poet's having compared the lady to Cleopatra. The queen in Shakespeare's drama – "Age cannot wither her, nor custom stale/Her infinite variety" – is perhaps the extreme exponent of love for love's sake, the feminine member of the pair of lovers who threw away an empire for love. But the infinite variety of the life of the woman in "A Game of Chess" *has* been staled. There is indeed no variety at all, and love simply does not exist. The function of the sudden change in the description of the carvings and paintings in the room from the heroic and magnificent to "and other withered stumps of time" is obvious. But the reference to Philomela is particularly important, for Philomela, it seems to me, is one of the major symbols of the poem.

Miss Weston points out (in *The Quest of the Holy Grail*) that a section of one of the Grail manuscripts, which is apparently intended to be a gloss on the Grail story, tells how the court of the rich Fisher King was withdrawn from the knowledge of men when certain of the maidens who frequented the shrine were raped and had their golden cups taken from them. The curse on the land follows from this act. Miss Weston conjectures that this may be a statement, in the form of a parable, of the violation of the older mysteries which were probably once celebrated openly, but were later forced underground. Whether or not Mr. Eliot noticed this passage or intends a reference, the violation of a woman makes a very good symbol of the process of secularization. John Crowe Ransom makes the point very neatly for us in *God Without Thunder*. Love is the aesthetic of sex; lust is the science. Love implies a deferring of the satisfaction of the desire; it implies a certain asceticism and a ritual. Lust drives forward urgently and sci- /147/ entifically to the immediate extirpation of the desire. Our contemporary waste land is in large part the result of our scientific attitude—of our complete secularization. Needless to say, lust defeats its own ends. The portrayal of "the change of Philomel, by the barbarous king" is a fitting commentary on the scene which it ornaments. The waste land of the legend came in this way; the modern waste land has come in this way.

This view is corroborated by the change of tense to which Edmund Wilson has called attention: "And still she *cried,* and still the world *pursues* [italics mine]." Apparently the "world" partakes in the barbarous king's action, and still partakes in that action.

To "dirty ears" the nightingale's song is not that which filled all the desert with inviolable voice—it is "jug,jug." Edmund Wilson has pointed out that the rendition of the bird's song here represents not merely the Elizabethans' neutral notation of the bird's song, but carries associations of the ugly and coarse. The passage is one, therefore, of many instances of Eliot's device of using something which in one context is innocent but in another context becomes loaded with a special meaning.

The Philomela passage has another importance, however. If it is a commentary on how the waste land became waste, it also repeats the theme of the death which is the door to life, the theme of the dying god. The raped woman becomes transformed through suffering into the nightingale; through the violation comes the "inviolable voice." The thesis that suffering is action, and that out of suffering comes poetry is a favorite one of Eliot's. For example, "Shakespeare, too, was occupied with the struggle—which alone constitutes life for a poet—to transmute his personal and private agonies into something rich and strange, something universal and impersonal." Consider also his statement with reference to Baudelaire: "Indeed, in his way of suffering is already a kind of presence of the supernatural and of the superhuman. He rejects always the purely nat- /148/ ural and the purely human; in other words, he is neither 'naturalist' nor 'humanist.'" The theme of the life which is death is stated specifically in the conversation between the man and the woman. She asks the question, "Are you alive, or not?" Compare the Dante references in "The Burial of the Dead."

(She also asks, "Is there nothing in your head?" He is one of the Hollow Men—"Headpiece filled with straw.") These people, as people living in the waste land, know nothing, see nothing, do not even live.

But the protagonist, after this reflection that in the waste land of modern life even death is sterile—"I think we are in rats' alley/ Where the dead men lost their bones"—remembers a death that was transformed into something rich and strange, the death described in the song from *The Tempest*—"Those are pearls that were his eyes."

The reference to this section of *The Tempest* is, like the Philomela reference, one of Eliot's major symbols. A general comment on it is therefore appropriate here, for we are to meet with it twice more in later sections of the poem. The song, one remembers, was sung by Ariel in luring Ferdinand, Prince of Naples, on to meet Miranda, and thus to find love, and through this love, to effect the regeneration and deliverance of all the people on the island. Ferdinand, hearing the song, says:

The ditty does remember my drowned father.
This is no mortal business, nor no sound
That the earth owes . . .

The allusion is an extremely interesting example of the device of Eliot's already commented upon, that of taking an item from one context and shifting it into another in which it assumes a new and powerful meaning. The description of a death which is a portal into a realm of the rich and strange—a death which becomes a sort of birth—assumes in the mind of the protagonist an association with that of the drowned god whose effigy was thrown into the water as a symbol of the death of the fruitful powers of nature but /149/ which was taken out of the water as a symbol of the revivified god. (See *From Ritual to Romance*.) The passage therefore represents the perfect antithesis to the passage in "The Burial of the Dead": "That corpse you planted last year in your garden," etc. It also, as we have already pointed out, finds its antithesis in the sterile and unfruitful death "in rats' alley" just commented upon. (We shall find that this contrast between the death in rats' alley and the death in *The Tempest* is made again in "The Fire Sermon.")

We have yet to treat the relation of the title of the second section, "A Game of Chess," to Middleton's play, *Women Beware Women,* from which the game of chess is taken. In the play, the game is used as a device to keep the widow occupied while her daughter-in-law is being seduced. The seduction amounts almost to a rape, and in a *double entendre,* the rape is actually described in terms of the game. We have one more connection with the Philomela symbol, therefore. The abstract game is being used in the contemporary waste land, as in the play, to cover up a rape and is a description of the rape itself.

In the latter part of "A Game of Chess" we are given a picture of spiritual emptiness, but this time, at the other end of the social scale, as reflected in the talk between two cockney women in a London pub. (It is perhaps unnecessary to comment on the relation of their talk about abortion to the theme of sterility and the waste land.)

The account here is straightforward enough, and the only matter which calls for comment is the line spoken by Ophelia in *Hamlet,* which ends the passage. Ophelia, too, was very much concerned about love, the theme of conversation between the women in the pub. As a matter of fact, she was in very much the same position as that of the woman who has been the topic of conversation between the two ladies whom we have just heard. And her poetry, like Philomela's, had come out of suffering. We are probably to look for the relevance of the allusion to her here rather than in an easy satiric contrast between Elizabethan glories /150/ and modern sordidness. After all, Eliot's criticism of the present world is not merely the sentimental one that this happens to be the twentieth century after Christ and not the seventeenth.

III

"The Fire Sermon" makes much use of several of the symbols already developed. The fire is the sterile burning of lust, and the section is a sermon, although a sermon by example only. This section of the poem also contains some of the most easily apprehended uses of literary allusion. The poem opens on a vision of the modern river. In Spenser's "Prothalamion" the scene described is also a river scene at London, and it is dominated by nymphs and their paramours, and the nymphs are preparing for a wedding. The contrast between Spenser's scene and its twentieth century equivalent is jarring. The paramours are now "the loitering heirs of city directors," and, as for the nuptials of Spenser's Elizabethan maidens, in the stanzas which follow we learn a great deal about those. At the end of the section the speech of the third of the Thames-nymphs summarizes the whole matter for us.

The waters of the Thames are also associated with those of Leman—the poet in the contemporary waste land is in a sort of Babylonian Captivity.

The castle of the Fisher King was always located on the banks of a river or on the sea shore. The title "Fisher King," Miss Weston shows, originates. from the use of the fish as a fertility or life symbol. This meaning, however, was often forgotten, and so his title in many of the later Grail romances is accounted for by describing the king as fishing. Eliot uses the reference to fishing for reverse effect. The reference to fishing is part of the realistic detail of the scene—"While I was fishing in the dull canal." But to the reader who knows the Weston references, the reference is to that of the Fisher King of the Grail legends. The protagonist is the maimed and impotent king of the legends. /151/

Eliot proceeds now to tie the waste-land symbol to that of *The Tempest*, by quoting one of the lines spoken by Ferdinand, Prince of Naples, which occurs just before Ariel's song, "Full Fathom Five," is heard. But he alters *The Tempest* passage somewhat, writing not, "Weeping again the king my father's wreck," but

Musing upon the king my brother's wreck
And on the king my father's death before him.

It is possible that the alteration has been made to bring the account taken from *The Tempest* into accord with the situation in the Percival stories. In Wolfram von Eschenbach's *Parzival*, for instance, Trevrezent, the hermit, is the brother of the Fisher King, Anfortas. He tells Parzival, "His name all men know as Anfortas, and I weep for him evermore." Their father, Frimutel, is dead.

The protagonist in the poem, then, imagines himself not only in the situation of Ferdinand in *The Tempest* but also in that of one of the characters in the Grail legend; and the wreck, to be applied literally in the first instance, applies metaphorically in the second.

After the lines from *The Tempest*, appears again the image of a sterile death from which no life comes, the bones, "rattled by the rat's foot only, year to year." (The collocation of this figure with the vision of the death by water in Ariel's song has already been commented on. The lines quoted from *The Tempest* come just before the song.)

The allusion to Marvell's "To His Coy Mistress" is of course one of the easiest allusions in the poem. Instead of "Time's winged chariot" the poet hears "the sound of horns and motors" of contemporary London. But the passage has been further complicated. The reference has been combined with an allusion to Day's "Parliament of Bees." "Time's winged chariot" of Marvell has not only been changed to the modern automobile; Day's "sound of horns and hunting" has changed to the horns of the motors. And Actaeon will not be brought face to face with Diana, god- /152/ dess of chastity; Sweeney, type of the vulgar bourgeois, is to be brought to Mrs. Porter, hardly a type of chastity. The reference in the ballad to the feet "washed in soda water" reminds the poet ironically of another sort of foot-washing, the sound of the children singing in the dome heard at the ceremony of the foot-washing which precedes the restoration of the wounded Anfortas (the Fisher King) by Parzival and the taking away of the curse from the waste land. The quotation thus completes the allusion to the Fisher King commenced in line 189 — "While I was fishing in the dull canal."

The pure song of the children also reminds the poet of the song of the nightingale which we have heard in "The Game of Chess." The recapitulation of symbols is continued with a repetition of "Unreal city" and with the reference to the one-eyed merchant.

Mr. Eugenides, the Smyrna merchant, is the one-eyed merchant mentioned by Madame Sosostris. The fact that the merchant is one-eyed apparently means, in Madame Sosostris' speech, no more than that the merchant's face on the card is shown in profile. But Eliot applies the term to Mr. Eugenides for a totally different effect. The defect corresponds somewhat to Madame Sosostris' bad cold. He is a rather battered representative of the fertility cults: the prophet, the *seer,* with only one eye.

The Syrian merchants, we learn from Miss Weston's book, were, along with slaves and soldiers, the principal carriers of the mysteries which lie at the core of the Grail legends. But in the modern world we find both the representatives of the Tarot divining and the mystery cults in decay. What he carries on his back and what the fortune-teller is forbidden to see is evidently the knowledge of the mysteries (although Mr. Eugenides himself is hardly likely to be more aware of it than Madame Sosostris is aware of the importance of her function). Mr. Eugenides, in terms of his former function, ought to be inviting the protagonist into the esoteric cult which holds the secret of life, but on the /153/ realistic surface of the poem, in his invitation to "a weekend at the Metropole" he is really inviting him to a homosexual debauch. The homosexuality is "secret" and now a "cult" but a very different cult from that which Mr. Eugenides ought to represent. The end of the new cult is not life but, ironically, sterility.

In the modern waste land, however, even the relation between man and woman is also sterile. The incident between the typist and the carbuncular young man is a picture of "love" so exclusively and practically pursued that it is not love at all. The tragic chorus to the scene is Tiresias, into whom perhaps Mr. Eugenides may be said to modulate, Tiresias, the historical "expert" on the relation between the sexes.

The fact that Tiresias is made the commentator serves a further irony. In *Oedipus Rex,* it is Tiresias who recognizes that the curse which has come upon the Theban land has been caused by the sinful sexual relationship of Oedipus and Jocasta. But Oedipus' sin has been committed in ignorance, and knowledge of it brings horror and remorse. The essential horror of the act which Tiresias witnesses in the poem is that it is not regarded as a sin at all — is perfectly casual, is merely the copulation of beasts.

The reminiscence of the lines from Goldsmith's song in the description of the young woman's actions after the departure of her lover, gives concretely and ironically the utter break-down of traditional standards.

It is the music of her gramophone which the protagonist hears "creep by" him "on the waters." Far from the music which Ferdinand heard bringing him to Miranda and love, it is, one is tempted to think, the music of "O O O O that Shakespeherian Rag."

But the protagonist says that he can *sometimes* hear "the pleasant whining of a mandoline." Significantly enough, it is the music of the fishermen (the fish again as a life symbol) and it comes from beside a church (though — if this is not to rely too much on Eliot's note — the church has been /154/ marked for destruction). Life on Lower Thames Street, if not on the Strand, still has meaning as it cannot have meaning for either the typist or the rich woman of "A Game of Chess."

The song of the Thames-daughters brings us back to the opening section of "The Fire Sermon" again, and once more we have to do with the river and the river-nymphs. Indeed, the typist incident is framed by the two river-nymph scenes.

The connection of the river-nymphs with the Rhine-daughters of Wagner's *Götterdämerung* is easily made. In the passage in Wagner's opera (to which Eliot refers in his note), the opening of Act III, the Rhine-daughters bewail the loss of the beauty of the Rhine occasioned by the theft of the gold, and then beg Siegfried to give them back the Ring made from this gold, finally threatening him with death if he does not give it up. Like the Thames-daughters they too have been violated; and like the maidens mentioned in the

Grail legend, the violation has brought a curse on gods and men. The first of the songs depicts the modern river, soiled with oil and tar. (Compare also with the description of the river in the first part of "The Fire Sermon.") The second song depicts the Elizabethan river, also evoked in the first part of "The Fire Sermon." (Leicester and Elizabeth ride upon it in a barge of state. Incidentally, Spenser's "Prothalamion" from which quotation is made in the first part of "The Fire Sermon" mentions Leicester as having formerly lived in the house which forms the setting of the poem.)

In this second song there is also a definite allusion to the passage in *Antony and Cleopatra* already referred to in the opening life of "A Game of Chess."

> Beating oars
> The stern was formed
> A gilded shell

And if we still have any doubt of the allusion, Eliot's note on the passage with its reference to the "barge" and "poop" /155/ should settle the matter. We have already commented on the earlier allusion to Cleopatra as the prime example of love for love's sake. The symbol bears something of the same meaning here, and the note which Eliot supplies does something to reinforce the "Cleopatra" aspect of Elizabeth. Elizabeth in the presence of the Spaniard De Quadra, though negotiations were going on for a Spanish marriage, "went so far that Lord Robert at last said, as I [De Quadra was a bishop] was on the spot there was no reason why they should not be married if the queen pleased." The passage has a sort of double function. It reinforces the general contrast between Elizabethan magnificence and modern sordidness: in the Elizabethan age love for love's sake has some meaning and therefore some magnificence. But the passage gives something of an opposed effect too: the same sterile love, emptiness of love, obtained in this period too: Elizabeth and the typist are alike as well as different. (One of the reasons for the frequent allusion to Elizabethan poetry in this and the preceding section of the poem may be the fact that with the English Renaissance the old set of supernatural sanctions had begun to break up. See Eliot's various essays on Shakespeare and the Elizabethan dramatists.)

The third Thames-daughter's song depicts another sordid "love" affair, and unites the themes of the first two songs. It begins "Trams

and *dusty* trees." With it we are definitely in the waste land again.
Pia, whose words she echoes in saying "Highbury bore me. Richmond
and Kew/Undid me" was in Purgatory and had hope. The woman
speaking here has no hope — she too is in the Inferno: "I can connect/
Nothing with nothing." She has just completed, floating down the
river in the canoe, what Eliot has described in *Murder in the
Cathedral* as

> . . . the effortless journey, to the empty land
> . . . .
> Where those who were men can no longer turn the mind /156/
> Where the soul is no longer deceived, for there are no objects,
>   no tones,
> To distraction, delusion, escape into dream, pretence,
> No colours, no forms to distract, to divert the soul
> From seeing itself, foully united forever, nothing with
>   nothing,
> Not what we call death, but what beyond death is not
>   death . . .

Now, "on Margate Sands," like the Hollow Men, she stands "on
this beach of the tumid river."

The songs of the three Thames-daughters, as a matter of fact,
epitomize this whole section of the poem. With reference to the
quotations from St. Augustine and Buddha at the end of "The Fire
Sermon" Eliot states that "the collocation of these two representatives of eastern and western asceticism, as the culmination of this
part of the poem, is not an accident."

It is certainly not an accident. The moral of all the incidents
which we have been witnessing is that there must be an asceticism
— something to check the drive of desire. The wisdom of the East
and the West comes to the same thing on this point. Moreover, the
imagery which both St. Augustine and Buddha use for lust is fire.
What we have witnessed in the various scenes of "The Fire Sermon"
is the sterile burning of lust. Modern man, freed from all restraints,
in his cultivation of experience for experience's sake burns, but not
with a "hard and gemlike flame." One ought not to pound the point
home in this fashion, but to see that the imagery of this section of
the poem furnishes illustrations leading up to the Fire Sermon is
the necessary requirement for feeling the force of the brief allusions
here at the end to Buddha and St. Augustine.

IV

Whatever the specific meaning of the symbols, the general function of the section, "Death by Water," is readily apparent. The section forms a contrast with "The Fire Ser- /157/ mon" which precedes it—a contrast between the symbolism of fire and that of water. Also readily apparent is its force as a symbol of surrender and relief through surrender.

Some specific connections can be made, however. The drowned Phoenician Sailor recalls the drowned god of the fertility cults. Miss Weston tells that each year at Alexandria an effigy of the head of the god was thrown into the water as a symbol of the death of the powers of nature, and that this head was carried by the current to Byblos where it was taken out of the water and exhibited as a symbol of the reborn god.

Moreover, the Phoenician Sailor is a merchant—"Forgot . . . the profit and loss." The vision of the drowned sailor gives a statement of the message which the Syrian merchants originally brought to Britain and which the Smyrna merchant, unconsciously and by ironical negatives, has brought. One of Eliot's notes states that the "merchant . . . melts into the Phoenician Sailor, and the latter is not wholly distinct from Ferdinand Prince of Naples." The death by water would seem to be equated with the death described in Ariel's song in *The Tempest*. There is a definite difference in the tone of the description of this death—"A current under sea/Picked his bones in whispers," as compared with the "other" death— "bones cast in a little low dry garret,/Rattled by the rat's foot only, year to year."

Further than this it would not be safe to go, but one may point out that whirling (the whirlpool here, the Wheel of Madame Sosostris' palaver) is one of Eliot's symbols frequently used in other poems (*Ash Wednesday,* "Gerontion," *Murder in the Cathedral,* and "Burnt Norton") to denote the temporal world. And I may point out, supplying the italics myself, the following passage from *Ash Wednesday:*

Although I do not hope to *turn* again

. . . .
Wavering between the *profit and the loss*
In this brief transit where the dreams cross
The dreamcrossed twilight *between birth and dying.* /158/

At least, with a kind of hindsight, one may suggest that "Death by Water" gives an instance of the conquest of death and time, the "perpetual recurrence of determined seasons," the "world of spring and autumn, birth and dying" through death itself.

V

The reference to the "torchlight red on sweaty faces" and to the "frosty silence in the gardens" obviously associates Christ in Gethsemane with the other hanged gods. The god has now died, and in referring to this, the basic theme finds another strong restatement:

> He who was living is now dead
> We who were living are now dying
> With a little patience

The poet does not say "We who *are* living." It is "We who *were* living." It is the death-in-life of Dante's Limbo. Life in the full sense has been lost.

The passage on the sterility of the waste land and the lack of water provides for the introduction later of two highly important passages:

> There is not even silence in the mountains
> But dry sterile thunder without rain —

lines which look forward to the introduction later of "what the thunder said" when the thunder, no longer sterile, but bringing rain, speaks.

The second of these passages is, "There is not even solitude in the mountains," which looks forward to the reference to the Journey to Emmaus theme a few lines later: "Who is the third who walks always beside you?" The god has returned, has risen, but the travelers cannot tell whether it is really he, or mere illusion induced by their delirium.

The parallelism between the "hooded figure" who "walks always beside you," and the "hooded hordes" is another instance of the sort of parallelism that is really a contrast. /159/ In the first case, the figure is indistinct because spiritual; in the second, the hooded hordes are indistinct because completely *unspiritual* — they are the people of the waste land —

> Shape without form, shade without colour,
> Paralysed force, gesture without motion —

to take two lines from "The Hollow Men," where the people of the waste land once more appear. Or to take another line from the same poem, perhaps their hoods are the "deliberate disguises" which the Hollow Men, the people of the waste land, wear.

Eliot, as his notes tell us, has particularly connected the description here with the "decay of eastern Europe." The hordes represent, then, the general waste land of the modern world with a special application to the breakup of Eastern Europe, the region with which the fertility cults were especially connected and in which today the traditional values are thoroughly discredited. The cities, Jerusalem, Athens, Alexandria, Vienna, like the London of the first section of the poem are "unreal," and for the same reason.

The passage which immediately follows develops the unreality into nightmare, but it is a nightmare vision which is something more than an extension of the passage beginning, "What is the city over the mountains" — in it appear other figures from earlier in the poem: the lady of "A Game of Chess," who, surrounded by the glory of history and art, sees no meaning in either and threatens to rush out into the street "With my hair down, so," has here let down her hair and fiddles "whisper music on those strings." One remembers in "A Game of Chess" that it was the woman's hair that spoke:

> . . . her hair
> Spread out in fiery points
> Glowed into words, then would be savagely still. /160/

The hair has been immemorially a symbol of fertility, and Miss Weston and Frazer mention sacrifices of hair in order to aid the fertility god.

As we have pointed out earlier, this passage is also to be connected with the twelfth chapter of Ecclesiastes. The doors "of mudcracked houses," and the cisterns in this passage are to be found in Ecclesiastes, and the woman fiddling music from her hair is one of "the daughters of musick" brought low. The towers and bells from the Elizabeth and Leicester passage of "The Fire Sermon" also appear here, but the towers are upside down, and the bells, far from pealing for an actual occasion or ringing the hours, are "reminiscent." The civilization is breaking up.

The "violet light" also deserves comment. In "The Fire Sermon" it is twice mentioned as the "violet hour," and there it has little more than a physical meaning. It is a description of the hour of twilight. Here it indicates the twilight of the civilization, but it is perhaps something more. Violet is one of the liturgical colors of the Church. It symbolizes repentance and it is the color of baptism. The visit to the Perilous Chapel, according to Miss Weston, was an initiation—that is, a baptism. In the nightmare vision, the bats wear baby faces.

The horror built up in this passage is a proper preparation for the passage on the Perilous Chapel which follows it. The journey has not been merely an agonized walk in the desert, though it is that; nor is it merely the journey after the god has died and hope has been lost; it is also the journey to the Perilous Chapel of the Grail story. In Miss Weston's account, the Chapel was part of the ritual, and was filled with horrors to test the candidate's courage. In some stories the perilous cemetery is also mentioned. Eliot has used both: "Over the tumbled graves, about the chapel." In many of the Grail stories the Chapel was haunted by demons.

The cock in the folk-lore of many people is regarded as the bird whose voice chases away the powers of evil. It is /161/ significant that it is after his crow that the flash of lightning comes and the "damp gust/Bringing rain." It is just possible that the cock has a connection also with *The Tempest* symbols. The first song which Ariel sings to Ferdinand as he sits "Weeping again the king my father's wreck" ends

> The strain of strutting chanticleer,
> Cry, cock-a-doodle-doo.

The next stanza is the "Full Fathom Five" song which Eliot has used as a vision of life gained through death. If this relation holds, here we have an extreme instance of an allusion, in itself innocent, forced into serious meaning through transference to a new context.

As Miss Weston has shown, the fertility cults go back to a very early period and are recorded in Sanscrit legends. Eliot has been continually, in the poem, linking up the Christian doctrine with the beliefs of as many peoples as he can. Here he goes back to the very beginnings of Aryan culture, and tells the rest of the story of the rain's coming, not in terms of the setting already developed but in its earliest form. The passage is thus a perfect parallel in method to the passage in "The Burial of the Dead":

> You who were with me in the ships *at Mylae*!
> That corpse you planted *last year* in your garden . . .

The use of Sanscrit in what the thunder says is thus accounted for. In addition, there is of course a more obvious reason for casting what the thunder said into Sanscrit here: onomatopoeia.

The comments on the three statements of the thunder imply an acceptance of them. The protagonist answers the first question, "What have we given?" with the statement:

The awful daring of a moment's surrender
Which an age of prudence can never retract
By this, and this only, we have existed. /162/

Here the larger meaning is stated in terms which imply the sexual meaning. Man cannot be absolutely self-regarding. Even the propagation of the race—even mere "existence"—calls for such a surrender. Living calls for—see the passage already quoted from Eliot's essay on Baudelaire—belief in something more than "life."

The comment on *dayadhvam* (sympathize) is obviously connected with the foregoing passage. The surrender to something outside the self is an attempt (whether on the sexual level or some other) to transcend one's essential isolation. The passage gathers up the symbols previously developed in the poem just as the foregoing passage reflects, though with a different implication, the numerous references to sex made earlier in the poem. For example, the woman in the first part of "A Game of Chess" has also heard the key turn in the door, and confirms her prison by thinking of the key:

Speak to me. Why do you never speak. Speak.
What are you thinking of? What thinking? What?
I never know what you are thinking. Think.

The third statement made by the thunder, *damyata* (control), follows the condition necessary for control, sympathy. The figure of the boat catches up the figure of control already given in "Death by Water"—"O you who turn the wheel and look to windward"—and from "The Burial of the Dead" the figure of happy love in which the ship rushes on with a fair wind behind it: *"Frisch weht der Wind . . ."*

I cannot accept Mr. Leavis' interpretation of the passage, "I sat upon the shore/Fishing, with the arid plain behind me," as meaning that the poem "exhibits no progression." The comment upon what the thunder says would indicate, if other passages did not, that the poem does "not end where it began." It is true that the protagonist does not witness a revival of the waste land; but there are two important relationships involved in his case: a personal one as well as a general one. If secularization has destroyed, /163/ or is likely to destroy, modern civilization, the protagonist still has a private obligation to fulfill. Even if the civilization is breaking up—"London Bridge is falling down falling down falling down"—there remains the personal obligation: "Shall I at least set my lands in order?" Consider in this connection the last sentences of Eliot's "Thoughts After Lambeth": "The World is trying the experiment of attempting to form a civilized but non-Christian mentality. The experiment will fail; but we must be very patient in awaiting its collapse; meanwhile redeeming the time: so that the Faith may be preserved alive through the dark ages before us; to renew and rebuild civilization, and save the World from suicide."

The bundle of quotations with which the poem ends has a very definite relation to the general theme of the poem and to several of the major symbols used in the poem. Before Arnaut leaps back into the refining fire of Purgatory with joy he says: "I am Arnaut who weep and go singing; contrite I see my past folly, and joyful I see before me the day I hope for. Now I pray you by that virtue which guides you to the summit of the stair, at times be mindful of my pain." This theme is carried forward by the quotation from *Pervigilium Veneris*: "When shall I be like the swallow." The allusion is also connected with the Philomela symbol. (Eliot's note on the passage indicates this clearly.) The sister of Philomela was changed into a swallow as Philomela was changed into a nightingale. The protagonist is asking therefore when shall the spring, the time of love, return, but also when will he be reborn out of his sufferings, and—with the special meaning which the symbol takes on from the preceding Dante quotation and from the earlier contexts already discussed—he is asking what is asked at the end of one of the minor poems: "When will Time flow away."

The quotation from "El Desdichado," as Edmund Wilson has pointed out, indicates that the protagonist of the poem has been disinherited, robbed of his tradition. The ruined tower is perhaps also the Perilous Chapel, "only the wind's /164/ home," and it is also the whole tradition in decay. The protagonist resolves to claim his tradition and rehabilitate it.

The quotation from *The Spanish Tragedy*—"Why then Ile fit you. Hieronymo's mad againe"—is perhaps the most puzzling of all these quotations. It means, I believe, this: The protagonist's acceptance of what is in reality the deepest truth will seem to the present world mere madness. ("And still she cried . . . 'Jug Jug' to dirty ears.") Hieronymo in the play, like Hamlet, was "mad" for a purpose. The protagonist is conscious of the interpretation which will be placed on the words which follow — words which will seem to many apparently meaningless babble, but which contain the oldest and most permanent truth of the race:

Datta. Dayadhvam. Damyata.

Quotation of the whole context from which the line is taken confirms this interpretation. Hieronymo, asked to write a play for the court's entertainment, replies:

Why then, I'll fit you; say no more.
When I was young, I gave my mind
And plied myself to fruitless poetry;
Which though it profit the professor naught,
Yet it is passing pleasing to the world.

He sees that the play will give him the opportunity he has been seeking to avenge his son's murder. Like Hieronymo, the protagonist in the poem has found his theme; what he is about to perform is not "fruitless."

After this repetition of what the thunder said comes the benediction:

Shantih   Shantih   Shantih

The foregoing account of *The Waste Land* is, of course, not to be substituted for the poem itself. Moreover, it certainly is not to be considered as representing *the method by which the poem was composed*. Much which the prose expositor /165/ must represent as though it had been consciously contrived obviously was arrived at unconsciously and concretely.

The account given above is a statement merely of the "prose meaning," and bears the same relation to the poem as does the "prose meaning" of any other poem. But one need not perhaps apologize for setting forth such a statement explicitly, for *The Waste Land* has been almost consistently misinterpreted since its first publication. Even a critic so acute as Edmund Wilson has seen the poem as essentially a statement of despair and disillusionment, and his account sums up the stock interpretation of the poem. Indeed, the phrase, "the poetry of drouth," has become a cliché of left-wing criticism. It is such a misrepresentation of *The Waste Land* as this which allows Eda Lou Walton to entitle an essay on contemporary poetry, "Death in the Desert"; or which causes Waldo Frank to misconceive of Eliot's whole position and personality. But more than the meaning of one poem is at stake. If *The Waste Land* is not a world-weary cry of despair or a sighing after the vanished glories of the past, then not only the popular interpretation of the poem will have to be altered but also the general interpretations of post-War poetry which begin with such a misinterpretation as a premise.

Such misinterpretations involve also misconceptions of Eliot's technique. Eliot's basic method may be said to have passed relatively unnoticed. The popular view of the method used in *The Waste Land* may be described as follows: Eliot makes use of ironic contrasts between the glorious past and the sordid present—the crashing irony of

> But at my back from time to time I hear
> The sound of horns and motors, which shall bring
> Sweeney to Mrs. Porter in the spring.

But this is to take the irony of the poem at the most superficial level, and to neglect the other dimensions in which it operates. And it is to neglect what are essentially more /166/ important aspects of his method. Moreover, it is to overemphasize the difference between the method employed by Eliot in this poem and that employed by him in later poems.

The basic method used in *The Waste Land* may be described as the application of the principle of complexity. The poet works in terms of surface parallelisms which in reality make ironical contrasts, and in terms of surface contrasts which in reality constitute parallelisms. (The second group sets up effects which may be described as the obverse of irony.) The two aspects taken together give the effect of chaotic experience ordered into a new whole, though the realistic surface of experience is faithfully retained. The complexity of the experience is not violated by the apparent forcing upon it of a predetermined scheme.

The fortune-telling of "The Burial of the Dead" will illustrate the general method very satisfactorily. On the surface of the poem the poet reproduces the patter of the charlatan, Madame Sosostris, and there is the surface irony: the contrast between the original use of the Tarot cards and the use made by Madame Sosostris. But each of the details (justified realistically in the palaver of the fortune-teller) assumes a new meaning in the general context of the poem. There is then, in addition to the surface irony, something of a Sophoclean irony too, and the "fortune-telling," which is taken ironically by a twentieth-century audience, becomes *true* as the poem develops—true in a sense in which Madame Sosostris herself does not think it true. The surface irony is thus reversed and becomes an irony on a deeper level. The items of her speech have only one reference in terms of the context of her speech: the "man with three staves," the "one-eyed merchant," the "crowds of people, walking round in a ring," etc. But transferred to other contexts they become loaded with special meanings. To sum up, all the central symbols of the poem head up here; but here, in the only section in which they are explicitly bound together, the binding is slight and accidental. The deeper lines of association only emerge in terms of the /167/ total context as the poem develops—and this is, of course, exactly the effect which the poet intends.

This transference of items from an "innocent" context into a context in which they become charged and transformed in meaning will account for many of the literary allusions in the poem. For example, the "change of Philomel" is merely one of the items in the decorative detail in the room in the opening of "A Game of Chess." But the violent change of tense—"And still she cried, and still the world pursues"—makes it a comment upon, and a symbol of, the modern world. And further allusions to it through the course of the poem gradually equate it with the general theme of the poem. The allusions to *The Tempest* display the same method. The parallelism between Dante's Hell and the waste land of the Grail legends is fairly close; even the equation of Baudelaire's Paris to the waste land is fairly obvious. But the parallelism between the death by drowning in *The Tempest* and the death of the fertility god is, on the surface, merely accidental, and the first allusion to Ariel's song is merely an irrelevant and random association of the stream-of-consciousness:

> Is your card, the drowned Phoenician Sailor,
> (Those are pearls that were his eyes. Look!)

And on its second appearance in "A Game of Chess" it is still only an item in the protagonist's abstracted reverie. Even the association of *The Tempest* symbol with the Grail legends in the lines

> While I was fishing in the dull canal
> . . . .
> Musing upon the king my brother's wreck

and in the passage which follows, is ironical merely. But the associations have been established, even though they may seem to be made in ironic mockery, and when we come to the passage, "Death by Water," with its change of tone, they assert themselves positively. We have a sense of /168/ revelation out of material apparently accidentally thrown together. I have called the effect the obverse of irony, for the method, like that of irony, is indirect, though the effect is positive rather than negative.

The melting of the characters into each other is, of course, an aspect of this general process. Elizabeth and the girl born at Highbury both ride on the Thames, one in the barge of state, the other supine in a narrow canoe, and they are both Thames-nymphs, who are violated and thus are like the Rhine-nymphs who have also been violated, etc. With the characters as with the other symbols, the surface relationships may be accidental and apparently trivial and they may be made either ironically or through random association or in hallucination, but in the total context of the poem the deeper relationships are revealed. The effect is a sense of the oneness of experience, and of the unity of all periods, and with this, a sense that the general theme of the poem is true. But the theme has not been imposed — it has been revealed.

This complication of parallelisms and contrasts makes, of course, for ambiguity, but the ambiguity, in part, resides in the poet's fidelity to the complexity of experience. The symbols resist complete equation with a simple meaning. To take an example, "rock" throughout the poem seems to be one of the "desert" symbols. For example, the "dry stone" gives "no sound of water"; woman in the waste land is "the Lady of the Rocks," and most pointed of all, there is the long delirium passage in "What the Thunder Said": "Here is no water but only rock," etc. So much for its general meaning, but in "The Burial of the Dead" occur the lines

> Only
> There is shadow under this red rock,
> (Come in under the shadow of this red rock).

Rock here is a place of refuge. (Moreover, there may also be a reference to the Grail symbolism. In *Parzival,* the /169/ Grail is a stone: "And this stone all men call the grail . . . As children the Grail doth call them, 'neath its shadow they wax and grow.") The paradox, life through death, penetrates the symbol itself.

To take an even clearer case of this paradoxical use of symbols, consider the lines which occur in the hyacinth girl passage. The vision gives obviously a sense of the richness and beauty of life. It is a moment of ecstasy (the basic imagery is obviously sexual); but the moment in its intensity is like death. The protagonist looks in that moment into the "heart of light, the silence," and so looks into — not richness — but blankness: he is neither "living nor dead." The symbol of life stands also for a kind of death. This duality of function may, of course, extend to a whole passage. For example, consider:

Where fishmen lounge at noon: where the walls
Of Magnus Martyr hold
Inexplicable splendour of Ionian white and gold.

The function of the passage is to indicate the poverty into which religion has fallen: the splendid church now surrounded by the poorer districts. But the passage has an opposed effect also: the fishmen in the "public bar in Lower Thames Street" next to the church have a meaningful life which has been largely lost to the secularized upper and middle classes.

The poem would undoubtedly be "clearer" if every symbol had a single, unequivocal meaning; but the poem would be thinner, and less honest. For the poet has not been content to develop a didactic allegory in which the symbols are two-dimensional items adding up directly to the sum of the general scheme. They represent drama-tized instances of the theme, embodying in their own nature the fundamental paradox of the theme.

We shall better understand why the form of the poem is right and inevitable if we compare Eliot's theme to Dante's and to Spenser's. Eliot's theme is not the state- /170/ ment of a faith held and agreed upon (Dante's *Divine Comedy*) nor is it the projection of a "new" system of beliefs (Spenser's *Faerie Queene*). Eliot's theme is the rehabilitation of a system of beliefs, known but now discredited. Dante did not have to "prove" his statement; he could assume it and move within it about a poet's business. Eliot does not care, like Spenser, to force the didacticism. He prefers to stick to the poet's business. But, unlike Dante, he cannot assume acceptance of the statement. A direct approach is calculated to elicit powerful "stock responses" which will prevent the poem's being *read* at all. Consequently, the only method is to work by indirection. The Christian material is at the center, but the poet never deals with it directly. The theme of resurrection is made on the surface in terms of the fertility rites; the words which the thunder speaks are Sanscrit words.

We have been speaking as if the poet were a strategist trying to win acceptance from a hostile audience. But of course this is true only in a sense. The poet himself is audience as well as speaker; we state the problem more exactly if we state it in terms of the poet's integrity rather than in terms of his strategy. He is so much a man of his own age that he can indicate his attitude toward the Christian tradition without falsity only in terms of the difficulties of a rehabilitation; and he is so much a poet and so little a propagandist that he can be sincere only as he presents his theme concretely and dramatically.

To put the matter in still other terms: the Christian terminology is for the poet a mass of clichés. However "true" he may feel the terms to be, he is still sensitive to the fact that they operate superficially as clichés, and his method of necessity must be a process of bringing them to life again. The method adopted in *The Waste Land* is thus violent and radical, but thoroughly necessary. For the renewing and vitalizing of symbols which have been crusted over with a distorting familiarity demands the type of organization which we have already commented on in dis- /171/ cussing particular passages: the statement of surface similarities which are ironically revealed to be dissimilarities, and the association of apparently obvious dissimilarities which culminates in a later realization that the dissimilarities are only superficial—that the chains of likeness are in reality fundamental. In this way the statement of beliefs emerges *through* confusion and cynicism—not in spite of them. /172/

"Difficulty in love is inseparable from the deracination and the alienation from which the international man suffers."

Delmore Schwartz

T. S. ELIOT AS THE INTERNATIONAL HERO

A culture hero is one who brings new arts and skills to mankind. Prometheus was a culture hero and the inventors of the radio may also be said to be culture heroes, although this is hardly to be confounded with the culture made available by the radio.

The inventors of the radio made possible a new range of experience. This is true of certain authors; for example, it is true of Wordsworth in regard to nature, and Proust in regard to time. It is not true of Shakespeare, but by contrast it is true of Surrey and the early Elizabethan playwrights who invented blank verse. Thus the most important authors are not always culture heroes, and thus no rank, stature, or scope is of necessity implicit in speaking of the author as a culture hero.

When we speak of nature and of a new range of experience, we may think of a mountain range: some may make the vehicles by means of which a mountain is climbed, some may climb the mountain, and some may apprehend the new view of the surrounding countryside which becomes possible from the heights of the mountain. T. S. Eliot is a culture hero in each of these three ways. This becomes clear when we study the relationship of his work to the possible experiences of modern life. The term, possible, should be kept in mind, for many human beings obviously disregard and turn

From "T. S. Eliot as the International Hero," *Partisan Review*, Vol. 12 (1945), 199-206. Reprinted by permission of the author and publisher.

their backs upon much of modern life, although modern life does not in the least cease to circumscribe and penetrate their existence.

The reader of T. S. Eliot by turning the dials of his radio can hear the capitals of the world, London, Vienna, Athens, Alexandria, Jerusalem. What he hears will be news of the agony of war. Both the agony and the width of this experience are vivid examples of how the poetry of T. S. Eliot has a direct relationship to modern life. The width and the height and the depth of modern life are exhibited in his poetry; the agony and the horror of modern life are represented as inevitable to any human being who does not wish to deceive himself with systematic lies. Thus it is truly significant that E. M. Forster, in writing of Eliot, should recall August 1914 and the beginning of /199/ the First World War; it is just as significant that he should speak of first reading Eliot's poems in Alexandria, Egypt, during that war, and that he should conclude by saying that Eliot was one who had looked into the abyss and refused henceforward to deny or forget the fact.

We are given an early view of the international hero in the quasi-autobiographical poem which Eliot entitles: "Mélange Adultère Du Tout." The title, borrowed from a poem by Corbière, is ironic, but the adulterous mixture of practically everything, every time and every place, is not ironic in the least: a teacher in America, the poem goes, a journalist in England, a lecturer in Yorkshire, a literary nihilist in Paris, overexcited by philosophy in Germany, a wanderer from Omaha to Damascus, he has celebrated, he says, his birthday at an African oasis, dressed in a giraffe's skin. Let us place next to this array another list of names and events as heterogeneous as a circus or America itself: St. Louis, New England, Boston, Harvard, England, Paris, the First World War, Oxford, London, the Russian Revolution, the Church of England, the post-war period, the world crisis and depression, the Munich Pact, and the Second World War. If this list seems far-fetched or forced, if it seems that such a list might be made for any author, the answer is that these names and events are *presences* in Eliot's work in a way which is not true of many authors, good and bad, who have lived through the same years.

Philip Rahv has shown how the heroine of Henry James is best understood as the heiress of all the ages. So, in a further sense, the true protagonist of Eliot's poems is the heir of all the ages. He is the descendant of the essential characters of James in that he is the American who visits Europe with a Baedeker in his hand, just like Isabel Archer. But the further sense in which he is the heir of all the ages is illustrated when Eliot describes the seduction of a typist in a London flat from the point of view of Tiresias, a character in a play by Sophocles. To suppose that this is the mere exhibition of learning or reading is a banal misunderstanding. The important point is that the presence of Tiresias illuminates the seduction of the typist just as much as a description of her room. Hence Eliot writes in his notes to *The Waste Land* that "what Tiresias *sees* is the substance of the poem." The illumination of the ages is available at any moment, and when the typist's indifference and boredom in the act of love must be represented, it is possible for Eliot to invoke and paraphrase a lyric from a play by Oliver Goldsmith. Literary allusion has become not merely a Miltonic reference to Greek gods and Old Testament geography, not merely the citation of parallels, but a powerful and /200/ inevitable habit of mind, a habit which issues in judgment and the representation of different levels of experience, past and present.

James supposed that his theme was the international theme: would it not be more precise to speak of it as the transatlantic theme? This effort at a greater exactness defines what is involved in Eliot's work. Henry James was concerned with the American in Europe. Eliot cannot help but be concerned with the whole world and all history. Tiresias sees the nature of love in all times and all places and when Sweeney outwits a scheming whore, the fate of Agamemnon becomes relevant. So too, in the same way exactly, Eliot must recognize and use a correspondence between St. Augustine and Buddha in speaking of sensuality. And thus, as he writes again in his notes to *The Waste Land,* "The collocation of these two representatives of eastern and western asceticism as the culmination of this part of the poem is not an accident." And it is not an accident that the international hero should have come from St. Louis, Missouri, or at any rate from America. Only an American with a mind and sensibility which is cosmopolitan and expatriated could have seen Europe as it is seen in *The Waste Land.*

A literary work may be important in many ways, but surely one of the ways in which it is important is in its relationship to some important human interest or need, or in its relationship to some new aspect of human existence. Eliot's work is important in relationship to the fact that experience has become international. We have become an international people, and hence an international hero is possible. Just as the war is international, so the true causes of many of the things in our lives are world-wide, and we are able to understand the character of our lives only when we are aware of all history, of the philosophy of history, of primitive peoples and the

Russian Revolution, of ancient Egypt and the unconscious mind. Thus again it is no accident that in *The Waste Land* use is made of *The Golden Bough*, and a book on the quest of the Grail; and the way in which images and associations appear in the poem illustrates a new view of consciousness, the depths of consciousness and the unconscious mind.

The protagonist of *The Waste Land* stands on the banks of the Thames and quotes the Upanishads, and this very quotation, the command to "give, sympathize, and control," makes possible a comprehensive insight into the difficulty of his life in the present. But this emphasis upon one poem of Eliot's may be misleading. What is true of much of his poetry is also true of his criticism. When the critic writes of tradition and the individual talent, when he declares /201/ the necessity for the author of a consciousness of the past as far back as Homer, when he brings the reader back to Dante, the Elizabethans and Andrew Marvell, he is also speaking as the heir of all the ages.

The emphasis on a consciousness of literature may also be misleading, for nowhere better than in Eliot can we see the difference between being merely literary and making the knowledge of literature an element in vision, that is to say, an essential part of the process of seeing anything and everything. Thus, to cite the advent of Tiresias again, the literary character of his appearance is matched by the unliterary actuality by means of which he refers to himself as being "like a taxi throbbing waiting." In one way, the subject of *The Waste Land* is the sensibility of the protagonist, a sensibility which is literary, philosophical, cosmopolitan and expatriated. But this sensibility is concerned not with itself as such, but with the common things of modern life, with two such important aspects of existence as religious belief and making love. To summon to mind such profound witnesses as Freud and D. H. Lawrence is to remember how often, in modern life, love has been the worst sickness of human beings.

The extent to which Eliot's poetry is directly concerned with love is matched only by the extent to which it is concerned with religious belief and the crisis of moral values. J. Alfred Prufrock is unable to make love to women of his own class and kind because of shyness, self-consciousness, and fear of rejection. The protagonists of other poems in Eliot's first book are men or women laughed at or rejected in love, and a girl deserted by her lover seems like a body deserted by the soul.

In Eliot's second volume of poems, an old man's despair issues in part from his inability to make love, while Sweeney, an antithetical character, is able to make love, but is unable to satisfy the woman with whom he copulates. In *The Waste Land,* the theme of love as a failure is again uppermost. Two lovers return from a garden after a moment of love, and the woman is overcome by despair or pathological despondency. A lady, perhaps the same woman who has returned from the garden in despair, becomes hysterical in her boudoir because her lover or her husband has nothing to say to her and cannot give her life any meaning or interest: "What shall I do now?" she says, "what shall I ever do?" The neurasthenic lady is succeeded in the poem by cockney women who gossip about another cockney woman who has been made ill by contraceptive pills taken to avoid the consequences of love; which is to say that the sickness of love has /202/ struck down every class in society: "What you get married for, if you don't want children?" And then we witness the seduction of the typist; and then other aspects of the sickness of love appear when, on the Thames bank, three girls ruined by love rehearse the sins of the young men with whom they have been having affairs. In the last part of the poem, the impossibility of love, the gulf between one human being and another, is the answer to the command to give, that is to say, to give oneself or surrender oneself to another human being in the act of making love.

ʟElsewhere love either results in impotence, or it is merely copulation. In "The Hollow Men," the hollow men are incapable of making love because there is a shadow which falls between the desire and the spasm. The kinship of love and belief is affirmed when the difficulty of love and of religious belief are expressed in the same way and as parallels, by means of a paraphrase and parody of the Lord's Prayer.⏌In "Sweeney Agonistes," Sweeney returns to say that that there is nothing in love but copulation, which, like birth and death, is boring. Sweeney's boredom should be placed in contrast with the experience of Burbank, who encountered the Princess Volupine in Venice, and found himself impotent with her. A comparison ought also to be made between Sweeney and the protagonist of one of Eliot's poems in French who harks back to a childhood experience of love: "I tickled her to make her laugh. I experienced a moment of power and delirium." Eliot's characters when they make love either suffer from what the psychoanalysts term "psychic impotence," or they make love so inadequately that the lady is left either hysterical or indifferent when the episode is over. The characters who are potent and insensitive are placed in contrast with the characters who are impotent and sensitive. Grishkin has a bust which promises pneumatic bliss, while Burbank's kind, the kind of a man who goes to Europe with a Baedeker, has to crawl between the dry ribs of metaphysics because no contact possible to flesh is satisfactory. The potent and the insensitive, such as Sweeney, are not taken in by the ladies, the nightingales and the whores; but Burbank, like Agamemnon, is betrayed and undone.

This synoptic recitation might be increased by many more examples. Its essence is expressed perfectly in "Little Gidding": "Love is the unfamiliar name." But we ought to remember that the difficulty of making love, that is to say, of entering into the most intimate of relationships, is not the beginning but the consequence of the whole character of modern life. That is why the apparatus of reference which the poet brings to bear upon failure in love involves all history /203/ ("And I Tiresias have foresuffered all") and is international. So too the old man who is the protagonist of "Gerontion" must refer to human beings of many nationalities, to Mr. Silvero at Limoges, Hakagawa, Madame de Tornquist, Fräulein von Kulp and Christ [the tiger] and he finds it necessary to speak of all history as well as his failure in love. History is made to illuminate love and love is made to illuminate history. In modern life, human beings are whirled beyond the circuit of the constellations: their intimate plight is seen in connection or relation with the anguish of the Apostles after Calvary, the murder of Agamemnon, the insanity of Ophelia and children who chant that London bridge is falling down. In the same way, the plight of Prufrock is illuminated by means of a rich, passing reference to Michelangelo, the sculptor of the strong and heroic man. Only when the poet is the heir of all the ages can he make significant use of so many different and distant kinds of experience. But conversely, only when experience becomes international, only when many different and distant kinds of experience are encountered by the poet, does he find it necessary to become the heir of all the ages.

Difficulty in love is inseparable from the deracination and the alienation from which the international man suffers. When the traditional beliefs, sanctions and bonds of the community and of the family decay or disappear in the distance like a receding harbor, then love ceases to be an act which is in relation to the life of the community, and in immediate relation to the family and other human beings. Love becomes purely personal. It is isolated from the past and the future, and since it is isolated from all other relationships, since it is not longer celebrated, evaluated and given a status by the community, love does become merely copulation. The protagonist of "Gerontion" uses one of the most significant phrases in Eliot's work when he speaks of himself as living in a

94

⌊ *rented* house; ·which is to say, not in the house where his forbears lived. He lives in a rented house, he is unable to make love, and he knows that history has many cunning, deceptive, and empty corridors. The nature of the house, of love and of history are interdependent aspects of modern life. ⌋   END

When we compare Eliot's poetry to the poetry of Valèry, Yeats and Rilke, Eliot's direct and comprehensive concern with the essential nature of modern life gains an external definition. Yeats writes of Leda and he writes of the nature of history; Valèry writes of Narcissus and the serpent in the Garden of Eden; Rilke is inspired by great works of art, by Christ's mother and by Orpheus. Yet in /204/ each of these authors the subject is transformed into a timeless essence. The heritage of Western culture is available to these authors and they use it many beautiful ways; but the fate of Western culture and the historical sense as such does not become an important part of their poetry. And then if we compare Eliot with Auden and with Pound, a further definition becomes clear. In his early work, Auden is inspired by an international crisis in a social and political sense; in his new work, he writes as a teacher and preacher and secular theologian. In neither period is all history and all culture a necessary part of the subject or the sensibility which is dealing with the subject. With Pound, we come closer to Eliot and the closeness sharpens the difference. Pound is an American in Europe too, and Pound, not Eliot, was the first to grasp the historical and international dimension of experience, as we can see in an early effort of his to explain the method of the *Cantos* and the internal structure of each *Canto:* "All times are contemporaneous," he wrote, and in the *Cantos,* he attempts to deal with all history as if it were part of the present. But he fails; he remains for the most part an American in Europe, and the *Cantos* are never more than a book of souvenirs of a tour of the world and a tour of culture.

To be international is to be a citizen of the world and thus a citizen of no particular city. The world as such is not a community and it has no constitution or government: it is the turning world in which the human being, surrounded by the consequences of all times and all places, must live his life as a human being and not as the citizen of any nation. Hence, to be the heir of all the ages is to inherit nothing but a consciousness of how all heirlooms are rooted in the past. Dominated by the historical consciousness, the international hero finds that all beliefs affect the holding of any belief (he cannot think of Christianity without remembering Adonis); he finds that many languages affect each use of speech (*The Waste Land* concludes with a passage in four languages).

When nationalism attempts to renew itself, it can do so only through the throes of war. And when nationalism in America attempts to become articulate, when a poet like Carl Sandburg writes that "The past is a bucket of ashes," or when Henry Ford makes the purely American remark that "History is the bunk," we have only to remember such a pilgrimage as that of Ford in the Peace Ship in which he attempted to bring the First World War to an end in order to see that anyone can say whatever he likes: no matter what anyone says, existence has become international for everyone.

Eliot's political and religious affirmations are at another extreme, /205/ and they do not resemble Ford's quixotic pilgrimage except as illustrating the starting-point of the modern American, and his inevitable journey to Europe. What should be made explicit here is that only one who has known fully the deracination and alienation inherent in modern life can be moved to make so extreme an effort at returning to the traditional community as Eliot makes in attaching himself to Anglo-Catholicism and Royalism. Coming back may well be the same thing as going away; or at any rate, the effort to return home may exhibit the same predicament and the same topography as the fact of departure. Only by going to Europe, by crossing the Atlantic and living thousands of miles from home, does the international hero conceive of the complex nature of going home.

Modern life may be compared to a foreign country in which a foreign language is spoken. Eliot is the international hero because he has made the journey to the foreign country and described the nature of the new life in the foreign country. Since the future is bound to be international, if it is anything at all, we are all the bankrupt heirs of the ages, and the moments of the crisis expressed in Eliot's work are a prophecy of the crises of our own future in regard to love, religious belief, good and evil, the good life and the nature of the just society. *The Waste Land* will soon be as good as new. /206/

part 3

SOME LATER CRITICS

"... *the theory and influence of Eliot* ... *seem to me the most dangerous and nearly the least defensible of our time. They have grown upon our time with all the benumbing energy of a bad habit* ..."

Yvor Winters, *The Anatomy of Nonsense* (Norfolk, 1943), p. 167.

"This is a general description of Imagist technique; it is . . . the procedure of The Waste Land. *. . . I cannot think that the problems raised by the structure of* The Waste Land *have been faced."*

Graham Hough

IMAGISM AND ITS CONSEQUENCES

Literature, by a fortunate dispensation, does not reflect very accurately the convulsions of the social order. Its revolutions sometimes precede the social ones, sometimes follow them, sometimes, it would seem, overlap them quite pointlessly. In any case the cultural historian has no difficulty in finding the relations he is disposed to find. He deals in large masses of material, the phenomena are so numerous that they can surely be connected in more ways than the ingenuity of a commentator can devise. But as soon as we begin to look closely at a particular patch of literature we are likely to see it developing according to its own principles, which have their own interest, and are likely to be at least partly fortuitous in their relations to the wars, technologies or movements of classes that are their temporal accompaniments. The dispensation is fortunate, for it is a happy instance of what we mean by the freedom of the spirit.

Looked at in a sufficiently apocalyptic light, the extraordinary outbreak of genius and novelty in the literature of the early part of this century can be seen as the response of the imagination to the appalling /1/ moral and political history of our age. And so no doubt it is, and all the books with crisis, revolt, dilemma and hazard in their titles are right. But part of the imaginative response has al-

From *Reflections on a Literary Revolution* by Graham Hough (Washington, D. C.: The Catholic University of America Press, 1960), Chapter I, "Imagism and Its Consequences," pp. 1-40, with notes, p. 126. Reprinted by permission of the publisher.

ways been to occupy itself with other things than crises and hazards. "I particularly admired your use of the pluperfect subjunctive" as Claudel once remarked to Gide. The imagination has its own procedures and its own stratagems, different for every art in which it expresses itself. In the visual arts and in music the devices may be of international range. In literature they can hardly be that, for each language has its own procedure, never held quite in common with that of any other. The closer we come to a particular literature the more closely its features will be seen to depend on the state of the language at the time, the state of previous writing in it, the prestige or the declining fortune of special forms. In short, a literary revolution must be a *literary* revolution if it is to be anything. It may accompany or be accompanied by almost any other kind of revolution, at almost any distance. But unless we are looking at literature as a symptom of something else (a possibly respectable occupation, but not that of the literary critic) what must be attended to is the behaviour of literature itself.

The years between 1910 and the second world war saw a revolution in the literature of the English language as momentous as the Romantic one of a century before. It is an Anglo-American development that is /2/ itself part of a whole European affair. Beside the names of Yeats, Joyce, Eliot and Pound we should wish to place those of Gide, Valéry and Thomas Mann, perhaps Proust and Rilke from an earlier generation. Here is our identification parade for the modern spirit in letters. But here too we have such a huge and various collective phenomenon that almost anything we care to say about it would be true of some part or other; the target is so large that any chance-aimed shot would be sure to hit it somewhere. If we look at it *en masse* we shall soon find ourselves speaking of crisis in Western values, of dissociation of sensibility, of alienation, and disinherited minds. Looking from this vertiginous height we shall surely be able to make many observations that are true, the more easily since they are not liable to the contradictions of particularity. Let us descend and recover balance by observing a fixed spot—London in the years just before 1914. It was there that the English cell of an almost world-wide poetic conspiracy was being incubated—the first plot against the literary establishment for over a hundred years. Of course foreign agents were at work; there had been correspondence with France and the Orient; a person from Idaho and one from St. Louis were actually present.

So in the next few years "modern poetry" came into being. Strangely, it is still modern poetry, the same article, sold under the same name. The revolution is /3/ long past. Of the central revolutionary quartet—Pound, Eliot, Joyce and Wyndham Lewis—"the men of 1914," as Lewis liked to call them (it is characteristic that the turn of phrase should be borrowed from European revolutionary politics) two are dead, one legally irresponsible, and the fourth is happily still with us, the greatest living man of letters. A generation has had to pass to bring about this change of aspect. But nothing has happened to dispute with their productions the title of modern letters. No *avant-garde* had advanced any farther. There is no *avant-garde*. When I was a boy "modern poetry" was to be distinguished from poetry simple. Poetry was inherited from parents and learnt at school; it was the "Ode on a Grecian Urn" and "The Solitary Reaper." Modern poetry was read in a different context; neither one's parents nor anyone at school knew anything about it. Modern poetry is now academically respectable. It is taught in college courses, and the exposition of it gives employment to many worthy persons. But it is still almost as distinct from "poetry" as ever. Distinct in the general imagination, and not only in that; even among those who seriously profess the arts there is a feeling of the discontinuity between the literature of our century and that of any previous one. The singularity of modern poetry, for example, is one of the arguments used by C. S. Lewis to support his hypothesis of a great rift in our culture just before the present age. /4/

This consciousness of modernity is a distinctively modern thing; it is largely the work of the revolutionary generation itself. Pound's essays were called *Make It New*. In the stream of advice and exhortation he offered to young writers there is a continual insistence on novelty and on being up-to-date. "No good poetry is ever written in a manner twenty years old." "The scientist does not expect to be acclaimed as a great scientist until he has *discovered* something."[1] In both his and Eliot's criticism we are always hearing about "what remains to be done," "what is to be done next." A curious instance of this acute period-consciousness occurs quite recently, in Mr. Eliot's introduction to Pound's *Literary Essays*. He cites as one of the tricks of malevolent critics—"to quote what a writer said twenty or thirty years ago as if it was something he had said yesterday."[2] It is hard to imagine Johnson or Coleridge or Arnold finding it "malevolent" to quote a twenty-year-old dictum without the appropriate date. Lest I be suspected of malevolence may I add that the date of this remark is 1954, a date far removed

---

[1]The notes for this essay are printed at the end of the article—*Editor's note.*

from the dust of revolutionary conflict. Plainly the instigators of the late poetic innovation were badly frightened by a Zeitgeist, and the effects have been lasting.

The new poetry was new in the twenties, and it is still new, in the sense that we have nothing newer. As early as 1935 we find Sir Herbert Read, in an /5/ essay called *Form in Modern Poetry,* complaining of backsliding, of a decline in revolutionary and experimental ardour. It might be that the new tradition had established itself, that we now have a body of followers working in an accepted mode. But this is not true, or true only in a very restricted area. The revolution of 1914 was quite as momentous as the Romantic one of over a century before, but it was different. The Romantic change was not at all antipathetic to ancient and deep-rooted tendencies. In many ways it was a return to them; the old textbook term is after all the Romantic Revival. The result is that its habits of feeling and expression are a model for the next hundred years. The nineteenth-century shelves are stuffed with Wordsworthian poems, Keatsian poems and Byronic poems. The modern revolution has had a different fate. In one direction, in the establishment of a modern colloquial poetic idiom, the younger writers have certainly learnt the lesson of their elder contemporaries. All that purgation of poetic diction that has been so carefully and beautifully worked out, both in theory and in practice, by Mr. Eliot has become an almost absolute critical rule. The rule has been formulated, with something less than complete approval, in a recent essay by John Crowe Ransom: "That is simply a bad poem whose unfashionable or dated diction the plain reader spots at the first reading." But other parts of the newly-conquered territory are being little culti- /6/ vated. A belated critical posse in full jungle kit still hacks its way through these no longer very forbidding areas, in the pages of the semi-academic reviews; and that is about all. The influence of the generation of 1914 was always of a peculiar kind. On taste, ideas and feelings about literature it was dynamic, radical, and in the end largely triumphant. A diluted version of Mr. Eliot's critical doctrine (and that includes, at one remove, a great deal of the doctrines of Hulme, Pound and Lewis) is by now the possession of undergraduates and schoolboys. Mr. Eliot's version of English literary history is as much an orthodoxy as Matthew Arnold's was a generation before. Yet the direct effect on literary practice has been strangely small. There is no other poem of any significance remotely like *The Waste Land;* the metrics and the ordonnance of Pound's *Propertius* have had no successors whatever; no one has ever seriously attempted to emulate Joyce's most characteristic experiments; and the extraordinary bundle of detestations that go to make up Wyndham Lewis are so arbitrary that they are a monument to nothing but himself.

A rich and vigorous body of literature has established itself, but has not established a workable tradition. A possibility (it has been faintly entertained by Mr. Blackmur)[3] is that it is not through this self-consciously "modern" literature that the main road runs; that these writers are not the transmitters of the most /7/ vigorous poetic life of our time. Perhaps the authentic torch has been borne by writers of a more traditional cast — shall we say by Robert Frost, Robert Graves and E. M. Forster? But this is not really a possibility. It is not the admirable workers in traditional modes who have given the twentieth century its peculiar kind of vitality. The suggestion is entertained only to be dismissed. As I show it to the door I become aware of one of its relatives faintly demanding admittance. Deep in the folk-memory of English literary critics is the echo of a time when it was possible to speak of something called "the English spirit." Few, in a state of full vigilance, would allow this faded trope to escape their lips now. But I intend to employ it, not meaning whatever Sir Arthur Quiller-Couch would have meant by it, but meaning something like the spirit of the language, the whole drift and pressure given by the whole body of poetry written in English. The suggestion that knocks at the door is that specifically "modern" poetry is hostile to this spirit and has tried to move against that pressure. A few very powerful talents succeeded in establishing idiosyncratic positions. No one since has been powerful enough to take up the same stance or sufficiently supple and adaptable to go back and take up the old path where it left off. This is at least plausible as far as English is concerned, though in America it may be less so. It need not surprise us when we consider that two of the "men of /8/ 1914" were Americans, one an Irishman, and the origins of the other shrouded in mystery.

The suggestion may be allowed to stand in the doorway, for we are not yet in a position to examine its credentials. We have not yet asked what the nature of the twentieth-century revolution is, so we cannot yet know how it is related to the English poetic tradition. It is notable that whatever was happening in those years has not yet acquired a name. Mr. Blackmur has referred to the whole European movement, with which the English one belongs, as Expressionism. I should not be very happy with this as far as our domestic affair is concerned. Expressionism in art has Germanic connotations, and the literature we are considering is Anglo-American profoundly influenced by France. And Expressionism is a name for a kind of critical doctrine, a doctrine of personality and self-expression, that is precisely the one *not* held by our twentieth century school. I should like to have a name; it is a nuisance not to have one for something one is always discussing; but I should prefer to look nearer home and hope to fare better.

If we look into the archives of the period of revolutionary preparation, the name that is going about is Imagism. A "school of images" is referred to. Ezra Pound announces that as for the future the "Imagistes" have that in their keeping. This was in a note to the complete poetical works of T. E. Hulme (five poems), /9/ published at the end of *Ripostes* in 1912. Several forms of an Imagist manifesto exist; and Ezra Pound's "A few don'ts by an Imagist" appeared in *Poetry* in 1913. And there are several Imagist anthologies, the first under the auspices of Ezra Pound, others under those of Amy Lowell. In the narrow sense, the name refers to a movement whose history was brief, broken and querulous, whose poetic results were minuscule. The refinement of our numbers was to be accomplished by the introduction of the *haiku*, the Japanese poem of seventeen syllables. The tongue that Milton spake is not easily compressed into seventeen-syllable units; and even in its longer flights Imagism remains a small affair. But as a centre and an influence it is not small. It is the hard irreducible core of a whole cluster of poetic ideas that extend far beyond Imagism as a movement. Imagist ideas are at the centre of the characteristic poetic procedures of our time, and there is a case for giving the word a wider extension.

Imagism sounds like a by-blow from Symbolism. Image and symbol — we have been pestered by both words long enough; often we do not distinguish between them. If we were talking about continental Europe instead of the Anglo-American literary world there would be no need to make much play with Imagism. Symbolism is already there, well established and more or less understood. There have been several attempts to see the new poetry in English simply as a /10/ part of this earlier European movement. Edmund Wilson sees it in this way, as a large extension of Symbolism, in *Axel's Castle*. But this justly famous book was written in the middle of the development that it describes, and has been overtaken by the event. Its introductory chapter on Symbolism seems thin today, though it was nourishing at the time. Sir Maurice Bowra, largely concerned with Europe, has written of modern literature as the heritage of Symbolism. More recently, Frank Kermode, in a brief, brilliant, unhistorical essay, *Romantic Image,* has conflated

Symbolism and Imagism, and even seen both of them as a continuation of the Romantic road. However, there is room for a distinction here, and not only room, but a real need for it.

Though Symbolism is in a sense a late development of Romantic thought it takes a decisively new turn. The great Romantic writers (Wordsworth, Coleridge, Keats) all see literature as deeply rooted in experience. The confessional poem, the truth that has been "proved" upon our pulses," the attitude of those "to whom the miseries of the world are misery and will not let them rest" — these are its characteristic expressions. Symbolism moves in the direction of an autonomous art, severed from life and experience by an impassable gulf. The Symbolists share with the Romantics the reliance on the epiphany, the moment of revelation; but they differ sharply about its status in nature and its rela- /11/ tion to art. Wordsworth's spiritual life is founded on such moments of illumination, and it is the business of his poetry both to describe them and to relate them to the whole experience of a long ordered lifetime. For the Symbolist poet there is no question of describing an experience; the moment of illumination only occurs in its embodiment in some particular artistic form. There is no question of relating it to the experience of a lifetime, for it is unique, it exists in the poem alone. Rimbaud's *alchimie du verbe* is not a mere phrase, for the poet not only transmits, he creates the revelations that make up his world.

Symbolism therefore has strong transcendental overtones. The poet is a magus, calling reality into existence. Or he is the sole transmitter of a mysterious system of correspondences that actually pervades the universe, but only becomes apparent in art. Or he is capable of evoking from the *Anima Mundi* symbols of the profoundest import, but strictly unexpoundable, for their content is inseparable from the form of their first expression. At times we seem to be in something like the medieval symbolic universe. But that symbolism has a key, a key given once and for all in revelation. Since the means of grace and some means of instruction are available to all, it was in a sense a joy in widest commonalty spread; while the Symbolist universe reveals itself only in glimpses, only in art, and only to initiates. /12/

Now while modern literature has been afflicted with a persistent hangover from the rich Symbolist symposium, the magical and transcendental pretensions of Symbolism have almost entirely disappeared. It is only in the work of the early Yeats that we can find the Symbolist doctrine in full bloom. Even here it is considerably contaminated with a non-literary occultism—theosophy, spiritualism, Madame Blavatsky and the order of the Golden Dawn. It is doubtful whether we can properly speak of a Symbolist movement in English poetry, in a historical sense. Of course, if we like to take Symbolism as a universal, recurrent phenomenon we can rope in such diverse figures as Blake and Herman Melville, and no doubt a dozen others, and make some use of the concept. I am speaking of Symbolism as a more or less dateable historical development, as the term is used in French literature. This development several times looks as though it is going to occur in English, but it never comes to much, though relations with the French movement were frequent and beguiling. There was a foreshadowing of French Symbolism in the Pre-Raphaelites; there were many importations of Symbolist doctrine in the nineties; but it is not until the years before the first world war that French doctrines and practice showed signs of giving rise to a new poetry in England.

The history is complicated, and it has still only partly been written. There are probably many reasons that /13/ Symbolism took such feeble roots in England. We had a little of it of our own already; English poetry lacks a Baudelaire to stand as *éminence grise* behind the movement; above all, Symbolist influence on sensibility was not paralleled by a close study of Symbolist forms. The *fin-de-siècle*, fertile in sentiments and attitudes that are important for modern literature, was curiously powerless to find forms to match them; and it was not until the years around 1910 that a radically new poetry, and that implies a new poetic form, really begins to appear in English. In those years, when the group that were later to call themselves Imagists were laying their plans, the transcendental pretensions of Symbolism were no longer easy to entertain. The career of Mallarmé had ended in silence and something like despair. *Un coup de dès jamais n'abolira le hasard.* Rimbaud's defection to slave-trading in Africa was itself a symbol of the inefficacy of magical Symbolism; and the innocuous chastities of Japanese poetry in dilute translation were focussing attention on the surface properties rather than on the mystic attributes of the symbol.

Certain aspects of Symbolist doctrine persist, but the nature of the attention is changed. Revelation becomes technique, incantation becomes a code of prohibitions. What emerges is a new phenomenon, to which we rightly give a new name—Imagism. Not to deal in definition at this stage, and in the hope that things /14/

will become clearer as we go on, we can describe it roughly as Symbolism without the magic. The symbol, naked and unexplained, trailing no clouds of glory, becomes the image.

Let us clip a few flowers from the imagist's garden of maxims:

An image is that which presents an intellectual and emotional complex in an instant of time.

Go in fear of abstractions.

The natural object is always the adequate symbol.

I believe that the proper and perfect symbol is the natural object, that if a man uses "symbols" he must so use them that their symbolic function does not obtrude; so that *a* sense, and the poetic quality of the passage, is not lost to those who do not understand the symbol as such, to whom, for instance, a hawk is a hawk.[4]

Unexceptionable sentiments, according to the canons of much modern poetics; but compare them with some pure symbolist pronouncements:

A symbol is indeed the only possible expression of some invisible essence, a transparent lamp about a spiritual flame.[5]

Je dis: une fleur! et, hors de l'oubli où ma voix relègue aucun contour, en tant que quelque chose d'autre que les calices sus, musicalement se lève, idée, même et suave, l'absente de tous bouquets.[6]

These alone will serve to illustrate the way the symbol has become *opaque* in transforming itself into the image. No transparent envelopes, or mysterious /15/ absences, or invisible essences. Direct treatment of the *thing,* we are told, is the great object. T. E. Hulme's early criticism hammers away at accurate description, hardness, clarity. And we know what came of it:

The apparition of these faces in the crowd;
Petals on a wet, black bough.[7]

Those dozens of little poems in Pound's *Ripostes* and later; clear, limited, without resonance, without transparency. "The natural object is always the adequate symbol"—but of what? Of nothing but itself. A world composed of atomic notations, each image separate from all the others. They neither lead into each other nor to apprehension on any other level. There is in all Pound's practice and theory at this time a positivism, a defiant insistence on the surface of things, and an insistence that the surface of things is all.

Pound writes of Laurent Tailhade:

> I think this sort of clear presentation is of the noblest tradition of our craft. It is surely the scourge of fools. It is what may be called the "prose tradition" of poetry, and by this I mean that it is a practice of speech common to good prose and good verse alike. . . . It means constatation of fact. It presents. It does not comment. . . . It is not a criticism of life. I mean it does not deal in opinion. It washes its hands of theories. It does not attempt to justify anybody's ways to anybody or anything else.[8]

But even Pound could not consistently maintain that the clear presentation of the object was the sole aim of /16/ poetry. Though he often talks in T. E. Hulme's terms, as though presentational accuracy was an end in itself, in other places the natural object is seen as the equivalent of an emotion. Poetry is the art of making equations for emotions. But it is an equation of which one side only is to be presented. Imagist convention forbids that most ancient recipe for a poem—the poem in which first a natural object is presented, and then some reflection on human experience that arises from it, or is in some way parallel to it. As a student of Provençal Pound must have been familiar with the *reverdie* and its long history—the spring song, whose first stanza presents "the soote sesoun that bud and bloom forth brings," whose later ones present the happy love that resembles it, or the unhappy love that contrasts with it. By his subsequent lights it is only possible for the poet to say "It is Spring"—and, unspoken, on no account to be uttered, only to be understood—"if you care to make any deductions from this to my state of mind, you may." But since the natural object is always the adequate symbol the poem will not make itself responsible for any of these deductions.

I leaned against a sturdy oak,
I thought it was a trusty tree;
But first it bent and syne it broke,
Sae did my true love lichtly me.

This is too explicit for true Imagist principles. The proper procedure
is to be seen in Pound's "Fan-Piece, /17/ for her Imperial Lord":

O fan of white silk,
        clear as the frost on the grass-blade,
You also are laid aside.[9]

So far, merely a change of rhetorical convention; a laconic
novelty of procedure that has its own charm. We know well enough
what the Imagists are tired of. They are tired of Arnold's "Dover
Beach"; the extended picture of the moonlight, the beach and the
tide; and then the inevitable, the too-long expected "The sea of
faith was once too at the full . . ."; the melancholy nineteenth-
century automatism by which no natural object can appear without
trailing its inglorious little cloud of moralising behind it. They
were right to be tired. One aspect of the history of poetry is an
intermittent warfare against automatisms, clichés of feeling and
expression. Only an intermittent warfare, for there are long periods
when poetry can rest, contented, healthy and active, within a set
of received conventions. But these periods come to an end. This was
a time when the battlefront had again become particularly active.

From this point of view Imagism was good tactics, and the
skirmish was conducted with vigour and address. But tactics are
not principles, and there is always danger when they are erected
into principles. Pound was particularly liable to make this trans-
formation. His insistence on procedure and technique is the /18/
beginning of this. "A few don'ts"; as though the writing of poetry
is the adroit employment of a series of gimmicks; the continual
invocation of "the expert"; the deference (in writing that shows
little deference) to the progress of the natural sciences:

What the expert is tired of to-day the public will be tired of
to-morrow.
It is not necessary that a poem should rely on its music,
but if it does rely on its music that music must be such as will
delight the expert.

The scientist does not expect to be acclaimed as a great scientist until he has *discovered* something. He begins by learning what has been discovered already. He goes from that point onward.

The best history of literature, more particularly of poetry, would be a twelve-volume anthology in which each poem was chosen . . . because it contained an invention, a definite contribution to the art of verbal expression.[10]

When Imagist doctrine was reinforced by Pound's study (if it can be called study) of Chinese, and his understanding (which was a misunderstanding) of the nature of Chinese ideogram, the gimmicks were well on the way to becoming a principle. When Pound took over Fenollosa's manuscripts he also took over the idea that the originally pictographic nature of the Chinese written character was still a subsistent force, that the reader actually *saw* the image in the complex ideogram. All scholars now agree that this is mistaken; even if they did not, it is on the face of it impossible; as impossible as to suppose that the reader of English /19/ resuscitates every dead metaphor as he goes along, thinks of weighing when he ponders, or of the stars when he considers. Even though it was untrue, this way of thinking might have given rise, when applied to an Indo-European language, to some sort of doctrine of radical metaphor—that poetry proceeds by distilling the quintessence of language. This, we have been told, is one of the keys to Mallarmé. But Pound shows no interest in this sort of speculation. His supposed nugget of wisdom from the East is used to provide a cultural foundation for the doctrine of the image. Chinese uses picture-writing and so ought we. A strain of crotchety hostility to the traditions of Western thinking begins to appear. An obscure ideological war is invented in which Confucius knocks out Aristotle and abstraction and discursive thought are left in ruins. Poetry proceeds by the juxtaposition of ideograms, and new ideogram is old image writ large. The unit of poetry is the pictograph, the record of a significant glimpse.

From then on the doctrine burgeons, flourishes, spreads its roots and sends up suckers in every direction. (Many of us have been suckers for it at one time or another.) It connects itself easily with other speculations and manoeuvres which start from a different point but begin to converge with Imagism. Joyce's "epiphany," the moment in which the essential nature of an object reveals itself, is presented with a good deal /20/ of Thomistic top-dressing; but it is really a survival from magical Symbolism, and our sense of this is confirmed by the *fin-de-siècle* prose in which the earlier Joycean epiphanies are often enshrined. The moment of revelation need not be a revelation of beauty or transcendence. The customs-house clock, Stephen tells Cranly, might suddenly be epiphanised—manifest itself in its essence.[11] Or more frequently, a quotidian object suddenly reveals not only its own nature, but that of the forces that went to make it, or of the whole circum-ambient situation: "one of those brown brick houses which seem the very incarnation of Irish paralysis." This can become something like a form of Imagist doctrine; more sophisticated, without the pinched prohibitory air that hangs round Imagism. It produces similar technical results—the instantaneous glimpse of a phenom-enal object as the basic symbolic counter. *Portrait of the Artist* is built out of a succession of such instants. Compared with the startling technical innovations of Joyce's later work its method is unsurprising. It is nevertheless one of the earliest examples of a narrative, a development, presented by a series of unlinked scenes or shots.

One of the most celebrated offshoots of the Imagist idea is Mr. Eliot's Objective Correlative. We are all heartily sick of the phrase, even Mr. Eliot, so I will only recall briefly its original formulation. "The only way of expressing emotion in the form of art is by /21/ finding an 'objective correlative'; in other words, a set of objects, a situation, a chain of events which shall be the formula of that *partic-ular* emotion; such that when the external facts, which must termi-nate in sensory experience, are given, the emotion is immediately evoked."[12] Objections have been made to the "expressionist" charac-ter of this passage—the suggestion that the business of the poet is to find external manifestations for previously determinate emotions. I wish to point to something rather different—the suggestion that the whole natural world offers to the poet a collection of bric-à-brac from which he takes selections to represent emotional states. "Direct presentation of the thing"—the image so produced exists to be one side of an equation the other side of which is an emotion. Plainly an eccentric view of the poet's procedure. We can hardly suppose that either the author of the *Iliad* or the author of

Christ, that my love was in my arms
And I in my bed again

were collecting *objets trouvés* in this way. Gerard Manley Hopkins wrote "The Wreck of the Deutschland" because he was moved by the account of a shipwreck in which five nuns were drowned; he did not go round looking for a suitable disaster to match an emotion that he already had. This is possibly a position that Mr. Eliot, who wrote of it a long time ago, would not wish to maintain in its full rigour. But we /22/ must in some sense hold him to it, for it has consequences in other parts of his thinking about poetry. There is the idea that coherence and validity of thought have nothing to do with poetic worth; Dante made great poetry out of a strong and beautiful philosophy, Shakespeare out of a muddled one, but this does not affect their merit as poets. There is the related idea that poets do not "think," they take over the thought of their time. This would make the poet's activity something like painting flowers on china plates that he had bought ready-made from the factory; and I am sure that this is not what Mr. Eliot means; but it is what he appears to be saying. There is the idea that meaning is a kind of sop thrown to the intellect, like the bit of meat the burglar keeps to give to the dog, while the "poetry" does its work.[13] These are all pervasive ideas in modern, post-symbolist poetic strategy, and they are all related to the root idea that the substance of poetry is the image and its resonances.

The doctrine has its corollary when we come to consider the major structure of poetry; one that is startlingly at variance with the classical view. If poetry is a matching up of images with emotions its underlying framework consists of emotions. Its order is therefore an order of emotions. In classical poetic theory (by classical I mean here one that prevailed generally from the Greeks till some time in the nineteenth century) the order of poetry was an order of events or /23/ thoughts. Events are capable of casual connection, thoughts of logical connection; the one is the structure of narrative or dramatic poetry, the other of philosophic or reflective poetry. Only in the briefest lyric can we find an order that is simply that of emotions; and classical poetic theory was not deduced from brief lyrics. One does not insist on an Aristotelian rigour of construction; but even in the looser forms the sense of a syntax of events or a syntax of thoughts is preserved; and criticism insisted on it. Emotions are not capable of such a syntax. A pattern can be made of them, by simple juxtaposition, but it will hardly be an integrated pattern, unless there runs through it the thread of narrative or logic. Imagist poetry has therefore been obliged to invoke *another kind of logic*, a logic of emotions that works in its own way, and is supposed to be especially suitable for poetry. The most compendious expression of this notion is to be found in Mr. Eliot's introduction to St. John Perse's *Anabase*:

> . . . any obscurity of the poem, on first readings, is due to the suppression of 'links in the chain,' of explanatory and connecting matter, and not to incoherence, or to the love of cryptogram. The justification of such abbreviation of method is that the sequence of images coincides and concentrates into one intense impression of barbaric civilisation. The reader has to allow the images to fall into his memory successively without questioning the reasonableness of each at the moment; so that, at the end, a total effect is produced.
>
> Such selection of a sequence of images and ideas has nothing chaotic about it. There is a logic of the imagi- /24/ nation as well as a logic of concepts. People who do not appreciate poetry always find it difficult to distinguish between order and chaos in the arrangement of images; and even those who are capable of appreciating poetry cannot depend upon first impressions. I was not convinced of Mr. Perse's imaginative order until I had read the poem five or six times. And if, as I suggest, such an arrangement of imagery requires just as much 'fundamental brainwork' as the arrangement of an argument, it is to be expected that the reader of a poem should take at least as much trouble as a barrister reading an important decision on a complicated case.[14]

This document is worth examining in some detail. The occasion is particular, but the application is general. What is outlined is the method of a school. Three layers are to be discerned in this ingenious piece of discourse. The first is simply descriptive. We are told of a "sequence of images," of images that fall into the memory successively with no question of reasonableness, of resultant obscurity. This is a general description of Imagist technique; it is the procedure of *Anabase*; it is also the procedure of *The Waste Land* and the *Cantos*. The second layer, interwoven with the first, but we are attempting to separate it, is one of justification. Two justifications of this method are in fact offered. They are not compatible with each other. The first is that any appearance of obscurity is merely due to the suppression of connecting matter: the logic of the poem is like the logic of any other kind of discourse, but it is presented in a concentrated and ellipti- /25/ cal form. The second justification, however, is that the poem is constructed according to a "logic of the imagination" which is different from ordinary logic. It requires as much effort as the construction of an argument, but it is evidently of a different kind. And besides these layers, of description and justification, there is a third layer of knock-me-down *argumentum ad hominem,* designed to cause alarm and despondency in the breasts of persons who have not yet accepted the first two. Such persons do not appreciate poetry, cannot distinguish between order and chaos, and, in their benighted triviality, have probably never thought of assimilating the action of a reader of poetry to that of a barrister getting up a brief.

There is much in this sort of argument that arouses suspicion. The device of dismissing one's opponents as unqualified instead of convincing them that they are wrong is one that works only with the very unsophisticated or the very easily scared. It has been greatly overworked by the founding fathers of modern poetics. Only poets can judge poetry; this is a matter for the expert; certificates of culture countersigned by Confucius, Lancelot Andrewes and Rémy de Gourmont to be produced on admission — but these minatory gestures have dwindled into a curious historic ritual; and they have been discussed elsewhere. A more serious question is whether the Imagist procedure here described is an ordinary mode of discourse telescoped /26/ and abbreviated, or whether some special "logic of the imagination" is involved.

Let us look at the organisation of *The Waste Land.* In detail, and in some places, the first explanation works well enough. The twenty opening lines of the poem can be seen as an elliptical narrative, with fragments of reflection and direct speech. ("April is the cruellest month. . . . [we] went on in sunlight, into the Hofgarten. . . . And when we were children, staying at the archduke's.") In principle it could be expanded, the links could be supplied; what we have is the natural result of the attempt at pruning and concentrating nineteenth-century poetic method. The sense of an existing but not definitely stated plot is still there. It will require a great deal more latitude to apply this argument to the major structure of the poem. We know now that it was of considerably greater length, and attained its present proportions under the direction of Ezra Pound. We have always known that "Death by Water," the Phlebas the Phoenician section, was not originally part of *The Waste Land,* since it is a translation from the French of the last section of an earlier poem "Dans le Restaurant." Its insertion was again due to Pound. We know too that "Gerontion" was at one time to be included but was in the end left out to become a separate poem.[15] If this is the logic of the imagination it is evidently patient of a good deal of outside influence. There is a /27/ curious fortuitousness about it. And mere ellipsis, the omission of connecting links, will not serve as an explanation of the changes of speaker, shifts in time, scene and mode of address, the liberation of the image from all continuity that give the poem its peculiarly coruscating surface. In the poem as a whole the sense of an unspoken underlying plot has completely disappeared.

I cannot think that the problems raised by the structure of *The Waste Land* have been faced. They have been a party matter, a matter for polemic or defence; they have been a shibboleth; to accept this sort of technique was at one time a sort of touchstone for participation in modern poetry. Above all, the methodological anfractuosities of the piece have fulfilled one of the main economic functions of poetry in this century—they have given employment to a host of scholiasts. But they have hardly been a matter for disinterested enquiry. While the poem was still capable of causing bewilderment it established itself. The brilliance of the imagery, the auditory and incantatory grandeur of its best passages, stole into the consciousness and became a part of our poetical property; it became ungrateful, almost indecent to ask of what sort of continuum these fragments were a part. And we became satisfied with a level of coherence that we should never have found sufficient in any earlier poem. The unity of emotional effect withdrew attention from the logical dis- /28/ continuity, the extraordinary rhetorical diversity. A poem about frustration, aridity, fear and the perversions of love—these signs were to be read by anyone. They were read, and in combination with the modern urban imagery they instigated the critics who said that the poem expressed "the disillusionment of a generation." For this, some years later, they were sternly reproved by the author; but they were no doubt expressing, in their way, the only sense they had of a unity of purpose in the poem. Meanwhile, prompted by the notes, many persons who had stopped reading *The Golden Bough* looked at it again, and those who had never heard of Miss Jessie Weston read *From Ritual to Romance*. None of them were bold enough to say in public that these studies did little to advance their understanding. Certainly they directed attention to recurring symbolism of death and rebirth, drought and rain. But this was the kind of pattern that in earlier poetry had been only secondary to structure of another kind; it could not be seen as constituting a structure in itself. So we turned to more peripheral matters. We looked up the quotations from Dante and Baudelaire, and our apprehension of isolated lines increased in depth. *Turdus aonalaschkae pallasii*, whose water-dripping song is justly celebrated, doubtless afforded satisfaction to many. And the volume of exegesis increased, the explanations that did not explain, the links that connected nothing to nothing. /29/ And by the time that the movement of modern poetry had gone far enough for it to be a possible object of contemplation and enquiry, one shrank from asking the real questions, lest what was after all one of the great poetic experiences of our time should be still further buried beneath yet another load of waste paper.

But the questions remain — above all the question of what really makes the poem a totality, if it is one at all. If we can imagine some ideal critic, acquainted with the poetical tradition of Europe, yet innocent of the spirit of our age, and if we can imagine ourselves persuading him to leave the question of total structure in abeyance, "to allow the images to fall into his memory successively without questioning the reasonableness of each" — he would still be struck by the extraordinary rhetorical incongruities. He would find within its four hundred lines passages that are narrative, others that are dramatic, descriptive, lyric, hallucinatory and allusive. The theory of genres was never watertight or exhaustive, but never before was there a poem of this length, or perhaps of any other length, in which the modes were so mixed. Nor is the rhetorical level any more constant than the rhetorical mode. A modern and highly individual elegiac intensity, pastiche Renaissance grandeur, sharp anti-thetical social comment in the Augustan manner, the low mimetic of public house conversation — all these and probably several other styles are found side by side. The relation /30/ of these is sometimes obvious; it is one of calculated contrast. But it is a question how hard such contrasts of texture can be worked in a relatively short poem without disastrous damage to the unity of surface. It is not so much in the obvious collisions of the high and the low styles that this is felt. That kind of calculated shock action is a limited effect, and the intention of producing the shock itself provides a medium between the two elements. It is the use of language in different and unrelated fashions in different parts of the poem that is disruptive. There is the lovely, romantically evocative manner of the hyacinth girl passage:

Yet when we came back, late, from the Hyacinth garden,
Your arms full, and your hair wet, I could not
Speak, and my eyes failed, I was neither
Living nor dead, and I knew nothing,
Looking into the heart of light, the silence.

These lines live unhappily in the same poem with:

Endeavours to engage her in caresses
Which still are unreproved, if undesired.
Flushed and decided, he assaults at once;
Exploring hands encounter no defence;
His vanity requires no response,
And makes a welcome of indifference.

The uneasiness does not arise from incompatibility of tone and feeling, but because the two passages are using language in utterly different ways; the first to evoke, by overtones and connotations, the trembling ghost of an intense emotion that is never located or /31/ defined; the second to define a situation by precise denotation and intelligent analysis. It is as though a painter were to employ a pointilliste technique in one part of a picture, and the glazes of the high renaissance in another.

When we come to the content of the separate passages the situation is disturbing in another way. It has become fashionable to refer to these contents as "themes," suggesting a vaguely musical analogy; and suggesting, too, I suppose, that the "themes" of a poem are related to each other only as the themes of a musical composition are. But themes in a poem are made of words, and words have meanings; our attention is never arrested at the verbal surface; it proceeds to what the words denote. They denote objects, persons and ideas; and it is very difficult altogether to dispel the notion that the objects, persons and ideas in a single poem should be in some intelligible relation to one another. A very little inspection of the commentaries, or questioning of readers of the poem, will show that this is not the case with *The Waste Land*; there is no certainty either about what is denoted, or how it is related to other denotations. It is sometimes suggested, for example, that the hyacinth girl is or might be the same as the lady who stayed with her cousin the archduke a few lines earlier. To me it has always been obvious that these fragmentary glimpses showed us, and were designed to show us, two different kinds of /32/ women and two different kinds of human relationship. I suppose that those who think otherwise have taken at least as much trouble and are no greater fools than I. And I see no means by which the matter could be decided.

We have already remarked that Phlebas the Phoenician had a prior existence in another context and was included by chance or outside suggestion. True, a place is rather arbitrarily prepared for him; Madame Sosostris the clairvoyant, who is supposed to be using a Tarot pack, produces the card of the drowned Phoenician sailor—which is not a member of the Tarot pack—in order to suggest in advance that Phlebas has some part in the structure of the poem. But what his part is remains quite uncertain. Here the commentators for the most part insist on resolutely marking time, for fear of committing themselves to a false step; and we are even bidden to observe that the "currents" which pick the drowned Phlebas's bones have a forerunner in the "currants" in the pocket of Mr. Eugenides the Smyrna merchant. Surely the last refuge of baffled imbecility.

It has been said that the poem adopts a "stream of consciousness" technique;[16] and this sounds reassuring without committing us to anything very much. But it is precisely what the poem does not do. The advantage of the "stream of consciousness" technique is that it allows a flood of images, more or less emancipated /33/ from narrative or logical continuity, while still preserving a psychological continuity—the continuity of inhering in a single consciousness. *The Waste Land* conspicuously forgoes this kind of unifying principle. One desperate expedient has been to fasten on Mr. Eliot's note to line 218: "Tiresias, although a mere spectator and not indeed a 'character,' is yet the most important personage in the poem, uniting all the rest. . . . What Tiresias *sees,* in fact, is the substance of the poem." In the light of this it can be suggested that the whole poem is Tiresias's "stream of consciousness."[17] This is probably to give the note more weight than it can bear, and in any case, it does little to the purpose. Who was Tiresias? A man who had also been a woman, who lived forever and could foretell the future. That is to say, not a single human consciousness, but a mythological catch-all, and as a unifying factor of no effect whatever.

I should like to commit myself to the view that for a poem to exist as a unity more than merely bibliographical, we need the sense of one voice speaking, as in lyric or elegiac verse; or of several voices intelligibly related to each other, as in narrative with dialogue or drama; that what these voices say needs a principle of connection no different from that which would be acceptable in any other kind of discourse; that the collocation of images is not a method at all, but the negation of method. In fact, to expose oneself com- /34/ pletely, I want to say that a poem, internally considered, ought to make the same kind of sense as any other discourse.

This should amount to a frontal attack on the main positions of modern poetics. I cannot feel that I have the equipment for this enterprise, nor if I had that it would be the right way to proceed. If the conviction I have baldly stated is just, its justice will be seen, in due time, not by virtue of a puny attack from a single criticaster, but by what Johnson calls the common sense of readers uncorrupted by literary prejudice. So I only wish to press my point in two directions of which I feel fairly certain, neither of them quite central.

For the first I return to the sentence of Johnson I have just quoted. "By the common sense of readers uncorrupted with literary prejudices, after all the refinements of subtlety and the dogmatism of learning, must be finally decided all claim to poetical honours." These are words that no one who cares about poetry in our century can read without a twinge. The appeal to a body of readers who are not specialists or eccentrics, who are merely representative of the common sentiment and intelligence of human kind, is one we feel ourselves so little able to make, one that we know so well, if we are honest, ought to be made — that we can think of it only with a feeling of distress. Where is contemporary poetry read, and where is it written? In the universities. Who reads it? Students; /35/ professional students of literature mostly, and professors, who expect to write papers on it, or to lecture on it — to "explicate" it, in the current technical cant. What has become (not to go back to some pre-lapsarian Eden) of the kind of public that even so recent a poet as Tennyson could enjoy? It has been warned off; it has been treated to sneers, threats and enigmas. It has been told so often that it has no status and no business in the sacred wood, and it has found the business actually being transacted there so remote from its ordinary apprehension, that it has turned away, in indifference, or disgust, or despair. A complex of social reasons is often produced to account for this; no doubt some of them are valid. A covert notion of social determinism is invoked to produce a sensation of comforting hopelessness about almost any undesirable situation today. But that is not my business. I am only concerned with what is intrinsic to poetry; and much of the reason for the narrow appeal of modern poetry is in the poetry itself. The wilful Alexandrianism, the allusiveness and multiplicity of reference, above all, the deliberate cultivation of modes of organisation that are utterly at variance with those of ordinary discourse – these are the main reasons for the disappearance of Johnson's common reader. It is hard to say this, for to say it lines one up with the hostile, the malicious and the Philistine, with all those who hate and suspect the exploring sensibility and have never made the attempt to /36/ penetrate into the imaginative life of their time. But it is sometimes necessary to risk being put in bad company for the sake of saying what seems to be true. One can only hope that one has better reasons for saying it.

For my second point I hope to produce a better reason. The poem that abandons the syntax of narrative or argument and relies on the interplay of "themes" or the juxtaposition of images according to the mysterious laws of poetic logic is not, so far as it is doing anything positive at all, doing anything that poetry has not done before. Clustered and repeated images, contrasts or echoes among them, a half-heard music of this kind has always been part of poetic effect. We have always partly known it, and modern criticism has done much to make it explicit. But in all poetry before our time this music has been background music. What we have heard with the alert and directed attention has been something different. It has been a story, or an argument, or a meditation, or the direct expression of feeling. Modern criticism has aroused our sense of this second sub-rational layer in our appreciation of poetry. Perhaps the most signal instance of this is the Shakespeare criticism of Wilson Knight, which sees the plays not as patterns made by character in action, but as "expanded metaphors," patterns of "themes" and "images." Modern poetry in the Imagist mode has performed the extraordinary manoeuvre of shifting its whole weight to this second level. It has shorn itself /37/ of paraphrasable sense, of all narrative or discursive line, and relies on the play of contrasted images alone. In doing so it has achieved a startling concentration and brilliance of the individual image, and a whole new rhetoric of its own, with its own special kind of fascination. I still wish to maintain that it is an inadequate rhetoric, inadequate for anything but very short poems and very special effects – states of madness and dream, for example. I take it that the case of Pound's *Cantos* goes without saying; they are the wreckage of poetry; brilliant passages, sometimes long, sometimes the merest splinters, floating in a turbid sea of stammering and incoherent mumble. But even in *The Waste Land* and the *Four Quartets*, where the level of the individual passages is far more consistent, and where it is just possible to give their arrangement some sort of publicly valid justification, the organising principle is still quite inadequate for poems of this scope. These poems survive, and will survive, not assisted by their structure, but in spite of it.

This is true of much of the work of Pound, Eliot and Wallace Stevens—to name three of the founding fathers of modern poetry. Their poetry suffers, even on the level on which it functions so persuasively and brilliantly, from the lack of any other level, the lack of public, explicit, paraphrasable discourse. We know, of course, about the "heresy of paraphrase" as it has been called—that we ought never to suppose that a /38/ paraphrase can tell us what a poem is "about." Perhaps we ought never to paraphrase a poem; but as with many other things that we ought never to do, we ought also to be able to feel that we could do it. The virtue that we exercise in not making a conceptual prose translation of a modern poem is generally a fugitive and cloistered virtue; for it would not be possible to give any such translation if we tried. To attempt to explain to an intelligent person who knows nothing about twentieth-century poetry how *The Waste Land* works is to be overcome with embarrassment at having to justify principles so affected, so perverse, so deliberately removed from the ordinary modes of rational communication. If poetry were to go on in this way it would develop before long into an esoteric entertainment with as much relevance to the experience of the common reader as, say, heraldry or real tennis. The imagist revolution was a sort of spring-cleaning; a much-needed spring-cleaning that got rid of a great deal of the fusty, obstructive and dust-gathering matter that had cluttered up the weaker poetry of the nineteenth century. But the house has not been comfortable to live in ever since. And the clotted rubbish of academic imagist criticism is already beginning to fill it up again. There is no reason to be optimistic about this situation. Poetry can degenerate into a meaningless esoteric exercise, and go on that way for centuries. It has happened. But perhaps it will not /39/ happen to us. And we have the example of the greatest poet of the early twentieth century to show that it need not. It is something of a paradox that Yeats, whose beliefs are often supposed to be more fantastic and irrational than those of any other great mind of our time, should never have lost his faith in rational order and the disposing intelligence as the guiding principle of a poem. /40/

NOTES

[1]*Literary Essays of Ezra Pound* (London, 1954), pp. 6,11.
[2]*Ibid.*, p. xi.

[3]R. P. Blackmur, *Anni Mirabiles 1921-25* (Washington, 1956), p. 41.

[4]*Literary Essays of Ezra Pound*, pp. 5, 9.

[5]W. B. Yeats, *Essays* (London, 1924), p. 142.

[6]Stéphane Mallarmé, *Œuvres Complètes* (Pleiade, Paris, 1945), p. 368.

[7]Copyright 1926 by Ezra Pound. Reprinted by permission of *New Directions*.

[8]"The Approach to Paris," *The New Age*, Oct. 2, 1913.

[9]Copyright 1926 by Ezra Pound. Reprinted by permission of *New Directions*.

[10]*Literary Essays of Ezra Pound*, pp. 5, 6, 17.

[11]James Joyce, *Stephen Hero* (New York, 1955), p. 210.

[12]"Hamlet and His Problems," *The Sacred Wood* (London, 1920), p. 100.

[13]T. S. Eliot, *The Use of Poetry and the Use of Criticism* (London, 1933), p. 151.

[14]From *Anabase* by St.-John Perse, translated by T. S. Eliot, copyright 1938, 1949, by Harcourt, Brace and Company, Inc., and reprinted with their permission. Throughout, the quotations from T. S. Eliot's *Collected Poems* (copyright 1936, by Harcourt, Brace and Company, Inc.) are used by permission of the publishers.

[15]See *Letters of Ezra Pound* (New York, 1950), pp. 169-172. It is also noteworthy that in John Rodker's circular for Bel Esprit, a proposed literary fund, *The Waste Land* is referred to as "a series of poems." (*Letters of Ezra Pound*, p. 175).

[16]Grover Smith, *T. S. Eliot's Poetry and Plays* (Chicago, 1956), p. 58.

[17]*Ibid.*, p. 58. See also George Williamson, *A Reader's Guide to T. S. Eliot* (New York, 1957), p. 123. /126/

"The Waste Land, *then, seems to me to work essentially against life, for the range of opinions it mobilises, that come welling up in response to it, are all negative.*"

David Craig

THE DEFEATISM OF *THE WASTE LAND*

T. S. Eliot's *The Waste Land* is one of the outstanding cases in modern times of a work which projects an almost defeatist personal depression in the guise of a full, impersonal picture of society. Lawrence's *Women in Love* is a much more substantial case of the same thing, but the response it demands is much less easy. Both, however, in my experience, encourage in readers, especially young students, a sort of superior cynicism which flatters the educated man by letting him feel that he is left as the sole bearer of a fine culture which the new mass-barbarians have spurned and spoiled. Eliot has characteristically slid out of responsibility in the matter by means of his remark that *The Waste Land* pleased people because of "their own illusion of being disillusioned".[1] But, I suggest, the essential (and very original) method of his poem and the peculiar sense of life which it mediates are such that they invite that very response – and get it from the most considerable critics as well as from young cynics.

Before considering *The Waste Land* itself, it will be as well to quote a case of that view of the modern 'plight' which the poem has licensed, or seemed sufficient grounds for. Summing up the social state of affairs which he sees as the basis for the poem's

From "The Defeatism of *The Waste Land*," *The Critical Quarterly,* ed. C. B. Cox and A. E. Dyson, Vol. II (1960), 241-252. Reprinted by permission of the author and publisher.
[1] T. S. Eliot, *Selected Essays* (ed. 1951), 'Thoughts after Lambeth', p. 368. /241/

'rich disorganisation', F. R. Leavis writes: "The traditions and cultures have mingled, and the historical imagination makes the past contemporary; no one tradition can digest so great a variety of materials, and the result is a break-down of forms and the irrevocable loss of that sense of absoluteness which seems necessary to a robust culture."[2] This is suggestive, and "that sense of absoluteness" implies a more felt idea of what modern rapid change has done to us than is usual in admirers of 'the organic community'. But consider what it leads on to:

In the modern Waste Land

> April is the cruellest month, breeding
> Lilacs out of the dead land,

but bringing no quickening to the human spirit. Sex here is sterile, breeding not life and fulfilment but disgust, accidia, and unanswerable questions. It is not easy today to accept the perpetuation and multiplication of life as ultimate ends.[3]

The logic of this is by no means consecutive: the critic is moving with shifts which seem not quite conscious, between life itself and the poem treated as a report on life. When he writes, "Sex here is sterile", although the immediate reference of 'here' seems to be the /241/ world of the poem, the quick shift to 'today', which must refer directly to real life here and now, suggests that Dr. Leavis considers the experience in *The Waste Land* a self-evident, perfectly acceptable version of the world we and the poet live in. That is the kind of assumption, and the pessimistic thought behind it, which I wish to challenge.

The technique of *The Waste Land* is very various; it gives the impression (compared with, say, Pound's *Cantos*) of rich, or intensely-felt, resources both of literature and of life direct. But one method stands out: that way of running on, with no marked break and therefore with a deadpan ironical effect, from one area of experience, one place or time or speech or social class, to another. Section II, 'A Game of Chess', throws shifting lights on the woman protagonist by changes of style. At first Cleopatra is present, but a Cleopatra who lives in an indoor, lifelessly ornate setting:

[2]*New Bearings in English Poetry* (ed. 1950), pp. 90-1. /241/
[3]*New Bearings*, p. 93. /241/

> The Chair she sat in, like a burnished throne,
> Glowed on the marble, where the glass
> Held up by standards wrought with fruited vines
> From which a golden Cupidon peeped out
> (Another hid his eyes behind his wing)
> Doubled the flame of sevenbranched candelabra
> Reflecting light upon the table as
> The glitter of her jewels rose to meet it . . .

By this point she has become Belinda from *The Rape of the Lock*, living in a world of 'things', make-up, dress, *bijouterie* — in Veblen's phrase, conspicuous consumption. But the modern poet does not have a mocking relish for the woman, as did Pope:

> This casket India's glowing gems unlocks,
> And all Arabia breathes from yonder box.
> The tortoise here and elephant unite,
> Transform'd to combs, the speckled and the white.
> Here files of pins extend their shining rows,
> Puffs, powders, patches, Bibles, billet-doux.

By the end of the equivalent passage in *The Waste Land*, the woman is not even Belinda, moving with assurance in her idle, expensive world. She is a neurotic who cannot stand being alone with her own thoughts — a type psychologically and socially akin to Eveline Hutchins who kills herself at the end of John Dos Passos's trilogy *U.S.A.* The change is given in the shift from a quite richly 'literary' diction —

> Under the firelight, under the brush, her hair
> Spread out in fiery points
> Glowed into words, then would be savagely still —

to a bitty, comparatively unshaped, modern spoken English (though the repetitiveness is cunningly stylised):

> 'My nerves are bad to-night. Yes, bad. Stay with me.
> 'Speak to me. Why do you never speak. Speak. /242/
>   What are you thinking of? What thinking? What?
> 'I never know what you are thinking. Think.'

The effect is of landing up with final disenchantment face to face with the unpleasant reality of life today.

There is then, in mid-section, a change of social class, from wealthy life ("The hot water at ten./And if it rains, a closed car at four") to ordinary ("When Lil's husband got demobbed, I said . . ."). But life is fruitless here too, and the poet's aloof revulsion is conveyed by similar means. The working-class women in the pub talk about false teeth, abortions, promiscuous sexual rivalry between the wives of Great War soldiers, in a lingo which sprawls over any kind of formal elegance of metre or rhyme; and the poet does not intrude on the common speech until the closing line:

Goonight Bill. Goonight Lou. Goonight May. Goonight
Ta ta. Goonight. Goonight.
Good night, ladies, good night, sweet ladies, good night,
    good night.

"Sweet ladies"—the irony is, to say the least, obvious. As well as the effect of 'sweet' there is the reminiscence of the innocently hearty student song (this seems more relevant than Ophelia's mad snatch in *Hamlet*). The effect is identical with what he does by incorporating Goldsmith's ditty from *The Vicar of Wakefield* at the end of the typist's dreary seduction in 'The Fire Sermon':

'Well now that's done: and I'm glad it's over.'
When lovely woman stoops to folly and
Paces about her room again, alone . . .

This technique, which is typical of the transitions of tone and of the collocation of two cultures which occur throughout the poem, seems to me unsatisfactory in two ways. The irony is no finer than ordinary sarcasm—the simple juxtaposing of messy reality and flattering description (as in a common phrase like "You're a pretty sight"). The pub women and the typist have been made so utterly sour and unlovely that the poet's innuendo, being unnecessary, does no more than hint at his own superior qualities. Secondly, using earlier literature to embody the better way of life which is the poet's ideal depends on a view of the past which is not made good in the poem (it hardly could be) and which the reader may well not share—unless he is pessimistic. Consider some further instances. The Thames as it is now is given thus at the beginning of 'The Fire Sermon':

Sweet Thames, run softly till I end my song.
The river bears no empty bottles, sandwich papers,

> Silk handkerchiefs, cardboard boxes, cigarette ends
> Or other testimony of summer nights . . .

The life evoked here is unpleasant — but so is the poet's attitude, notably the pointed but prudishly or suggestively tacit hint at contraceptives. At the same time, for us to respond as the poet /243/ means, we have to accept his glamourising view of Spenser's London, Elizabethan England with its pure rivers and stately ways. The same suggestion occurs in the lyrical passage which is meant to parallel the Rhinemaidens' song from *Götterdämerung*. Modern:

> The river sweats
> Oil and tar
> The barges drift
> With the turning tide . . .
> The barges wash
> Drifting logs
> Down Greenwich reach
> Past the Isle of Dogs.

Renaissance:

> Elizabeth and Leicester
> Beating oars
> The stern was formed
> A gilded shell
> Red and gold
> The brisk swell
> Rippled both shores . . .

The poet's meaning is clear: modern civilisation does nothing but spoil what was once gracious, lovely, ceremonious, and natural.

Here it must be said that the poet's comparative view of old and modern culture is not quite one-sided. As Hugh Kenner suggests, it may not be implied that Spenser's nymph-world "ever existed except as an ideal fancy of Spenser's"[1], and as Cleanth Brooks suggests, the Elizabeth passage has "a sort of double function": historically, Elizabeth flirted so wantonly with Leicester, in the presence of the Spanish bishop de Quadra, that Cecil at last

---

[1]*The Invisible Poet: T. S. Eliot* (New York, 1959), p. 165. /244/

suggested that as there was a bishop on the spot, they might as well be married there and then (Froude's *Elizabeth*, quoted in Eliot's note). As Brooks says, the passage "reinforces the general contrast between Elizabethan magnificence and modern sordidness: in the Elizabethan age love for love's sake has some meaning and therefore some magnificence. But the passage gives something of an opposed effect too: the same sterile love, emptiness of love, obtained in this period too: Elizabeth and the typist are alike as well as different."[2] In the whole poem, however, it is certainly old magnificence which is given the advantage, and it is as well to say straight out that this is an absurdly partial outlook on culture — groundlessly idealising about the old and warped in its revulsion from the modern. If magnificence is desired, modern life can supply it well enough, whether the show of Royalty or big-business ostentation. And if one thinks of the filth, poverty, superstition, and brutal knockabout life /244/ invariable in town or country four centuries ago, one realises how fatuous it is to make flat contrasts between then and now. History, reality, are being manipulated to fit an escapist kind of prejudice, however detached the writer may feel himself to be.

As one would expect, the cultural warp has as strong an equivalent in the poet's way of presenting personal experience. Consider the attitudes implied in the seduction of the typist. In this most cunningly-managed episode, one is induced to feel, by means of the fastidiously detached diction and movement, that a scene part commonplace, part debased, is altogether unpleasant. The experience is a more intimate meeting between people than Eliot deals with directly anywhere else in his work, but here is the style he finds for it:

> He, the young man carbuncular, arrives,
> A small house agent's clerk, with one bold stare,
> One of the low on whom assurance sits
> As a silk hat on a Bradford millionaire.
> The time is now propitious, as he guesses,
> The meal is ended, she is bored and tired,
> Endeavours to engage her in caresses
> Which still are unreproved, if undesired.
> Flushed and decided, he assaults at once;

---

[2]Cleanth Brooks, Jr., '*The Waste Land:* An Analysis': *Southern Review* (Louisiana State University, Summer 1937), Vol. 3, No. 1, p. 123. /244/

> Exploring hands encounter no defence;
> His vanity requires no response,
> And makes a welcome of indifference.

The unfeeling grossness of the experience is held off at the finger-
tips by the analytic, unphysical diction – "Endeavours to engage her
in caresses" – and by the movement, whose even run is not inter-
rupted by the violence of what is 'going on'. The neat assimilation
of such life to a formal verse paragraph recalls Augustan modes.
But if one thinks of the sexual passage concerning the 'Imperial
Whore' in Dryden's translation of Juvenal's sixth Satire, or even
the one concerning the unfeeling Chloe in Pope's *Moral Essay* 'Of
the Characters of Women',[1] one realises that the Augustans did
not stand off from the physical with anything like Eliot's distaste.
Eliot's style is carefully impersonal; it enumerates with fastidious
care the sordid details:

> On the divan are piled (at night her bed)
> Stockings, slippers, camisoles, and stays.

But here one has doubts. This is given as a typically comfortless
modern apartment, suggesting a life which lacks the right pace,
the right sociableness, the right instinctive decency for it to merit
the name of civilisation. (Were Elizabethan houses and habits any
better?) But the touch in the second line feels uncertain: is the
heavily careful art with which the line is built up not too contrived
/245/ for the rather ordinary modern habit it is meant to satirise?
When we come to 'carbuncular' – an adjective which, placed after the
noun and resounding in its slow movement and almost ornamental
air, is deliberately out of key with the commonplace life around it –
I think we begin to feel that Eliot's conscious literariness is working,
whatever his intention, more to hold at arm's length something
which he personally shudders at than to convey a poised criticism
of behaviour.[1] There is a shudder in 'carbuncular'; it is disdainful,
but the dislike is disproportionately strong for its object; queasy

[1]Dryden, 'The Sixth Satyr' of Juvenal, 11. 161-189; Pope, 'Of the Characters of Women', 11 157-
70. /245/
[1]Compare Lawrence's analysis of Thomas Mann: "Thomas Mann, like Flaubert, feels vaguely
that he has in him something finer than ever physical life revealed. Physical life is a disordered
corruption against which he can fight with only one weapon, his fine aesthetic sense, his feeling
for beauty, for perfection, for a certain fitness which soothes him, and gives him an inner pleasure, however corrupt the stuff of life may be . . . And so, with real suicidal intention,
like Flaubert's, he sits, a last too-sick disciple, reducing himself grain by grain to the statement
of his own disgust, patiently, self-destructively, so that his statement at least may be perfect in
a world of corruption." (See *Phoenix*, ed. Edward D. Macdonald, 1936, p. 312). /246/

emotions of the writer's seem to be at work.[2] The snobbery is of a piece with this. "He is a nobody – a mere clerk, and clerk to a *small* house agent at that. What right has *he* to look assured?" That is the suggestion; and we are also left wondering what warrant the poet has for uniting himself with some class finer, it seems, than the provincial bourgeoisie. And the passage ends with the snatch of Goldsmith, "When lovely woman stoops to folly":

She smoothes her hair with automatic hand,
And puts a record on the gramophone.

Here the nerveless movement and the ordinariness of the detail are deftly managed. And the human poverty of the scene has never been in doubt. But the writer's means of conveying *his valuation* of it are surely objectionable. One may agree or not that modern civilisation has its own kind of health; one may agree or not that the petty bourgeoisie are a decent class. But one must surely take exception to a method which seeks its effects through an irony which is no more than smart sarcasm. It is amazing that Dr. Leavis should speak of "delicate collocations",[3] when the contrasts are regularly so facile in their selection of old grandeur and modern squalor.

To put the matter in terms which refer directly to life: if, as Brooks says, "the same sterile love, emptiness of love, obtained in this period too", then why does the criticism work so consistently against contemporary civilisation? And when Dr. Leavis says, "Sex here is sterile", does he really mean that love between men and women has deteriorated as a whole? (One remembers similar extraordinary suggestions about intercourse now and formerly in *Lady Chatterley's Lover*.) The historian tells us that in Renaissance England, /246/

Wife-beating was a recognised right of man, and was practised without shame by high as well as low. Similarly, the daughter who refused to marry the gentleman of her parents' choice was liable to be locked up, beaten, and flung about the room, without any shock being inflicted on public opinion. Marriage was not an affair of personal affection but of family avarice, particularly in the 'chivalrous' upper classes.[1]

[2]Compare "The young are red and pustular" (from 'Mr. Eliot's Sunday Morning Service': *Collected Poems*, 1909-1935, ed. 1946, p. 53). /246/
[3]*New Bearings*, p. 112. /246/
[1]G. M. Trevelyan, *A Shortened History of England* (Pelican ed., 1959), p. 196. /247/

I think we may take it that the comparison of cultures to the advantage of the older is either impossible, pointless, or else feasible only by specific fields and not overall.[2] The question remains why critics have surrendered so gratefully to an almost nastily despairing view of the civilisation we live in. This occurs in Leavis's *New Bearings* and Edmund Wilson's *Axel's Castle*.[3] It is seen at its most irresponsible in Hugh Kenner's glib explication of the pub scene: "If we move from the queens to the pawns, we find low life no more free or natural, equally obsessed with the denial of nature, artificial teeth, chemically procured abortions, the speaker and her interlocutor battening fascinated at second-hand on the life of Lil and her Albert, Lil and Albert interested only in spurious ideal images of one another."[4] "Battening fascinated at second-hand" means no more than 'listening with interest to the tale of someone else's experiences': Mr. Kenner's condemnation comes from the general atmosphere of moral depression which the poem generates rather than from anything established by the dramatic speech of that scene—here the critic's sourness outdoes the poet's. And the reference to false teeth, lumped with abortions, as though false teeth were not simply an admirable achievement of medical science in giving comfort where nature has broken down, is a glaring case of that blind dislike of science which nowadays has become an intellectual's disease. It is primitivist; and it thoughtlessly ignores the experience involved.

Dr. Leavis's adherence to the old culture is much more scrupulously worked out, and must be considered by itself. A key term in that part of *New Bearings* (as in his early *Scrutiny* editorials) is 'continuity':

> In considering our present plight we have also to take account of the incessant rapid change that characterises the Machine Age. The result is breach of continuity and the uprooting of life. This last metaphor has a peculiar aptness, for what we are witnessing today is the final uprooting /247/ of the immemorial ways of life, of life rooted in the soil . . . There are ways in which it is possible to be too conscious; and to be so is, as a result

[2]An interesting suggestion has been made by the Communist Party Historians' Group that, as it is desirable that history should be taught as "matter of cause and effect, and, too, of human progress; as opposed to the view that history has nothing to teach, no meaning nor pattern", it should be taught through the history of technique "because progress in this field is clear . . . there is never total retrogression". ("The Teaching of History". *Marxism Today,* January 1959, p. 30). /247/

[3](New York, 1936), p. 106. /247/

[4]*The Invisible Poet,* p. 156. /247/

of the break-up of forms and the loss of axioms noted above, one of the troubles of the present age . . . [1]

Now, it would be foolish to burke the truth that the rapid disruption started by the Industrial Revolution undermined, and actually demoralised, the masses who were uprooted from the country and flung into the towns. But there are ways and ways of viewing this change—defeatist ways and constructive ways. The description of the old village culture which opens Engels's *Condition of the Working Class in England in 1844*[2] is remarkably similar to the main 'line' of *Scrutiny*; it belongs to the same humane tradition of protest at the harrow of industrialism. But realisation of such sufferings and social deterioration may lead on to a practical will to reconstruct, using the new social instruments, or it may lead on to a really helpless fixation on the past which comes from a distaste for the raw difficulties and uncomelinesses of the life around us. An outlook which assumes the fineness of the older culture belongs to the defeatist class. Dr. Leavis of course cannot back up his assumptions in a book mainly on modern poetry. But if we are to keep our thought grounded, we must notice that the obverse could be stated to every one of the advantages he sees in the 'organic' culture. Marx and Engels no doubt went too far the other way when they referred summarily to "the idiocy of rural life".[3] But when we speak of immemorial ways of life, we must remember how cramped a range of vocations they offered: consider the release of wider human talents made possible by the growth of technology and of organisation (both treated as evils by the *Scrutiny* critics). The village life was socially healthy in various ways, but it also ground down people cruelly: consider the lives of Burns and Gorky. When 'axioms' are mentioned, we must remember that they reflected fixed habits which held human possibilities in rigid bounds. I have suggested that it is futile to draw up an overall comparison between the old and contemporary types of culture. This is partly because we are now as we are; we have the means we now have; it is these alone that we can use. Therefore the only positive course is to co-operate with the hopeful present trends. No-one saw more piercingly into the anti-human effects of industrial labour as it once was than Marx; but he knew that that was the very means by which we must win through to the *new* good life. He gives this

[1]*New Bearings*, pp. 91, 93-4. /248/
[2]See Marx and Engels *On Britain* (Moscow, 1953), pp. 35-8. /248/
[3]*The Manifesto of the Communist Party* (Moscow, 1957), p. 55. /248/

balance of possibilities in passages such as these from *Capital*, vol.1:

> Modern Industry, on the other hand, through its catastrophes imposes the necessity of recognising, as a fundamental law of production, /248/ variation of work, consequently fitness of the labour for varied work, consequently the greatest possible development of his varied aptitudes . . . Modern Industry, indeed, compels society, under penalty of death, to replace the detail-worker of today, crippled by lifelong repetition of one and the same trivial operation, and thus reduced to the mere fragment of a man, by the fully developed individual, fit for a variety of labours, ready to face any change of production, and to whom the different social functions he performs, are but so many modes of giving free scope to his own natural and acquired powers:

(As a step towards this he then cites the setting up of agricultural and technical schools.) And again:

> However terrible and disgusting the dissolution, under the capitalist system, of the old family ties may appear, nevertheless, modern industry, by assigning as it does an important part in the process of production, outside the domestic sphere, to women, to young persons, and to children of both sexes, creates a new economical foundation for a higher form of the family and of the relations between the sexes . . . the fact of the collective working group being composed of individuals of both sexes and all ages, must necessarily, under suitable conditions, become a source of humane development . . . [1]

The Waste Land, then, seems to me to work essentially against life, for the range of opinions it mobilises, that come welling up in response to it, are all negative. In the final section Eliot uses the philosophy of F. H. Bradley. The lines

> I have heard the key
> Turn in the door once and turn once only
> We think of the key, each in his prison
> Thinking of the key, each confirms a prison . . .

he himself glosses from Bradley's *Appearance and Reality*:

[1] Trans. Moore and Aveling (New York, Modern Library), pp. 534, 536. /249/

My external sensations are no less private to myself than are my thoughts or my feelings. In either case my experience falls within my own circle, a circle closed on the outside; and with all its elements alike, every sphere is opaque to the others which surround it . . . In brief, regarded as an existence which appears in a soul, the whole world for each is peculiar and private to that soul.[2]

This thought of Bradley's has led on to that barren line of philosophy which includes John Wisdom's *Other Minds*. To say what must suffice here: if our sensations, thoughts, and feelings are perfectly private and the sphere of each person's life 'opaque', how is it that speech and literature themselves are intelligible — and intelligible so fully and intimately that to reach understanding with a person or appreciate a piece of writing can seem to take us inside another existence? That the question of whether one mind can get through to /249/ another should even have arisen seems to me a perversion of thought. (Historically, it is perhaps a cast from the anti-co-operative state of existence brought about by entrepreneur capitalism. It seems similar to the helplessly solipsistic "denial of objective truth" which Lenin refutes in *Materialism and Empirio-Criticism*. In each case the individual ego relies less and less on anything outside itself.)

The obscurity of *The Waste Land* is significant likewise, for though the trained reader no longer jibs at it, it is certainly impossible that it should ever become popular reading as did earlier important literature (Burns, Byron, George Eliot, D. H. Lawrence). Dr. Leavis writes on the issue of 'minority culture' which this raises: "that the public for it is limited is one of the symptoms of the state of culture which produced the poem. Works expressing the finest consciousness of the age in which the word "high-brow' has become current are almost inevitably such as to appeal only to a tiny minority".[1] The argument that follows is dubious at a number of points. In the first place, Lawrence expressed many sides of the "finest consciousness of the age" and he has been read in cheap editions by the million (as has Gorky in the Soviet Union and James T. Farrell in the United States). The usual obstinately pessimistic reply is that 'They only read Lawrence for the sex, or the love story'. But this is only reaching for another stick to beat the times, for is it not good that a major writer should have devoted himself to the universal subjects of love and sex? Dr. Leavis goes on to say

[2]Note to 1.411: *Collected Poems*, p. 84. /249/
[1]*New Bearings*, p. 104. /250/

that the idea that the poem's obscurity is symptomatic of our cultural condition "amounts to an admission that there must be something limited about the kind of artistic achievement possible in our time". But if this were so, how account for the work of Lawrence and of the many other considerable novelists of our time? Finally his question "how large in any age has the minority been that has really comprehended the masterpieces?" contains an equivocation—'really'. If one sets the highest standard, of course 'real' (that is, full) comprehension is attained by few; but if the numbers of even the *total* public reached are small, as has happened with *The Waste Land,* then there is indeed a significant difference between its meaningfulness and appeal for readers and that which the major novelists have regularly achieved (George Eliot, Hardy, Lawrence, Tolstoy, Gorky, Farrell). *The Waste Land,* in short, is *not* the representative work of the present age, and to make it so implies that pessimistic view of the present age which I have already challenged.

What has been made of *The Waste Land* illustrates two more issues important in our times. It is significant that Dr. Leavis should meet the charge that the poem is a 'dead end', literarily and morally. When he says, "So complete and vigorous a statement of the Waste Land could hardly . . . forecast an exhausted and hopeless sojourn /250/ there",[1] he implies a proper distinction between Eliot's quality of art and that of Pound's *Cantos* or Joyce's *Ulysses*—both recognisably from the same line of art distorted by the break-up of cultural forms. *The Waste Land,* it is true, does not cut life into bits and juggle them into patterns interesting only for their intricacy, or meaningful only to their manipulator. At the same time there turns out to be little that Dr. Leavis can plead convincingly when he has to say what way beyond the Waste Land Eliot found. He quotes some bracing sermons from the *Criterion:* "a tendency—discernible even in art—towards a higher and clearer conception of Reason, and a more severe and serene control of the emotions by Reason," and "the generation which is beginning to turn its attention to an athleticism, a *training,* of the soul as severe and ascetic as the training of the body of a runner".[2] The vague 'dedication' of this recalls the loftiness with no definite direction which characterised the more serious of the *fin de siècle* writers, notably Yeats, when they were being Hellenic or religiose. Its abstractness, its lack of reference to any social facts, suggests Eliot's inveterate drift away from any-

[1] *New Bearings,* pp. 113-4. /251/
[2] *Ibid.,* p. 114. /251/

thing progressive in society with which he might have co-operated in a practical way.[3]

The wider affiliations of such defeatism come out in the agreement Eliot and Leavis reach on 'eastern Europe'. Eliot's note introducing the final section of the poem says: "In the first part of Part V three themes are employed: the journey to Emmaus, the approach to the Chapel Perilous (see Miss Weston's book) and the present decay of eastern Europe".[4] This is very bland. The final phrase has that characteristic air of stating the unanswerable—he would explain further if he wished but he does not condescend to. Actually it must have behind it the most reactionary politics. How did Bela Kun's Communist régime in Hungary, for example, represent decay? or is Eliot sympathising with the Russian Tsars?[5] Dr. Leavis's interpretation is still more unacceptable: "These "hooded hordes', 'ringed by the flat horizon only', are not merely Russians, suggestively related to the barbarian invaders of civilisation . . ."[6] Eliot's poem, we need only recall, was being written when the civilised armies of Britain, America, France, and Japan were invading Russia on /251/ twenty-three fronts.[1] But there is nothing with which the pessimistic liberal *can* associate himself—neither the new civilisation which is being founded in the East nor the ordinary life of the West which he is so ready to write off.[2] /252/

---

[3]Compare Edmund Wilson's sensible criticism of Eliot's set of reactionary slogans, Royalist, classicist, and Anglo-Catholic: see 'T. S. Eliot and the Church of England', *The Shores of Light* (1952), [pp. 437-41.] /251/

[4]*Collected Poems*, p. 82. /251/

[5]Various touches suggest that he moves naturally amongst upper-class émigrés, e.g.:
Bin gar Keine Russin, stamm' aus Litauen, echt deutsch.
And when we were children, staying at the arch-duke's . . .
(Section I: *Poems*, p. 61) /251/

[6]*New Bearings*, p. 101. /251/

[1]This episode is summarised and placed by R. Palme Dutt in his *World Politics, 1918-1936* (1936), pp. 45-6. /252/

[2]Compare L. C. Knights, who argues straight from the debased mass media to the mentality of the people themselves: "Those Elizabethans who never got beyond Deloney, even those who remembered nothing of *King Lear* beyond the action and a couple of bawdy jokes, were not doomed to pass their lives in the emotional and intellectual muddledom of the readers of the *Daily Mail*." ('Elizabethan Prose': see *Drama and Society in the Age of Jonson*, ed. 1951, pp. 313-4). /252/

The Waste Land *"was very shortly made the sacred cow of modern poetry and the object of more pious literary nonsense than any modern work save the* Cantos *of Pound."*

Karl Shapiro

THE DEATH OF LITERARY JUDGMENT

There is no passable essay on Eliot at this time (about A.D. 1960) and little chance of there being one. As far as the literary situation goes, nothing could be more useful today, but the literary situation has seen to it that this essay does not exist. The very idea of a summary of Eliot's writings seems a kind of blasphemy, or an act of unpardonable rudeness. For the Literary Situation (whatever that ecclesiastical expression is supposed to mean) is largely Eliot's invention, and for that reason it is all but impossible to discuss. Eliot is untouchable; he is Modern Literature incarnate and an institution unto himself. One is permitted to disagree with him on a point here or a doctrine there, but no more. The enemy at Eliot's gate—practically everybody—searches his citadel for an opening and cannot find one. Eliot has long since anticipated every move; he and his men can prevent ingress or exit. Eliot resembles one of those mighty castles in Bavaria which are remarkably visible, famed for their unsightliness, and too expensive to tear down. Life goes on at the bottom; but *it* is always up there. /35/

The question of Eliot as the chief obstacle to poetry today may not be a real question; it may be precisely the kind of imaginary question which Eliot himself brings up in his writing. Insofar as one tries to deal with it, he is simply playing Eliot's game, with all the odds against him. I do not myself consider the question real, but I know of no way to discuss the ultimate value of Eliot's work without first discussing the exploits of his straw men. Eliot's reputation and the antagonism to it may be false. I propose in this essay to show both the reputation and the opposition to it in another light. That there is something of value in Eliot's poetry and Eliot's criticism is quite possible, even from my pessimistic point of view; though the valuable portion is miniscule and is much different from what has been supposed.

Eliot is both the hero and the victim of a historical predicament. And he himself is as much the author of that predicament as "history" itself. Eliot created a literary situation deliberately; he and his "situation" are fabrications, and very plausible fabrications at that. In other words, Eliot invented a Modern World which exists only in his version of it; this world is populated by Eliot's followers and is not a reality. The Eliot population consists of a handful of critics and professors and a few writers of Eliot's generation, though one would think, reading modern criticism and teaching from modern literary textbooks, that there really is a kingdom of Modern Poetry in which T. S. Eliot is the absolute monarch and Archbishop of Canterbury in one.

You will be thinking that I am using metaphorical language and am attempting to work up a nice critical discussion, the subject of which is the overestimation of T. S. Eliot. I am saying something quite different, namely, that Eliot exists only on paper, only in the /36/ minds of a few critics. No poet with so great a name has ever had less influence on poetry. At no point in the career of Eliot has there been the slightest indication of a literary following. For example, W. H. Auden, for a decade or so, set patterns for poetry which were followed by thousands of new poets all over the world. Dylan Thomas did the same, as did Wallace Stevens. Neither Eliot nor Pound ever had any such effect on their readers or on young writers. Eliot's "influence" is confined purely to criticism. Insofar as Eliot has enjoyed a *poetic* influence, it lies outside literature entirely and is what can only be called a "spiritual" influence. This spiritual influence is itself calculated and synthetic; and insofar as it fails as a true influence, it removes Eliot's one and only claim to literary power. But here he does not entirely fail.

To deal with Eliot outside the literary situation which he has invented, means to deal with his poetry head-on. It means passing judgment upon it as good or bad poetry or, in some cases, as not poetry at all. But how is one to look at Eliot, if not from his own viewpoint? There is the rub. Eliot has arranged matters in such a way that criticism of his own poetry is impossible.

Eliot has written a small body of poetry which is sacrosanct; he has written his most favorable criticism about poetry which is like his (namely Pound's); and has surrounded both with a full-scale esthetic-social doctrine. What I would like to do is to draw attention to Eliot's poetry—for that is the heart of the matter. For those who do not instinctively and spontaneously reject this poetry, I suppose some form of argument is required. Perhaps this essay will be of some assistance to them. I have in mind students primarily, those who are given Modern Poetry as gospel; I also /37/ have the young critic in mind, and also teachers and scholars. Poets do not need these remarks. I have met hundreds of poets in my life but not more than one or two who entertained the reverence for Eliot which they find in the textbooks. As most poets are not intellectuals and are the opposite, they are always stunned by the intellectual pretensions of Eliot and are at a loss to deal with them.

Eliot's preparation of the historical ground upon which he would found his position was the territory of all literature— excluding the Chinese, which was the preserve of Pound. He did not, evidently, intend a personal seizure of intellectual power; Eliot's famous humility testifies to his uneasiness in the face of over-whelming success. His irrational and subservient association with Pound also points to a genuine desire to refuse intellectual leader-ship, or at least to share it with others.

There was, it appears, a need for an Eliot about 1910. Eliot arrived on the literary scene at the point of vacuum; and he filled this vacuum which literary Nature abhors. Such at least is the accepted view. What is probably nearer the truth is that Eliot appeared at a time when the vitality of the audience was low; and when this is the case, criticism pours into the void. It is the critic in the guise of poet that we have to deal with, not a new kind of poet. For it is criticism which is the twentieth-century substitute for poetry.

The Historical Situation which Eliot exploits under the banner of Tradition was in the beginning the Educational Situation. It was local and Anglo-American, a defense of the Gentleman's Education. I put it vulgarly because that is the way it was. Too many writers have commented on Eliot's fears of being taken for a provincial for me to add my comment. /38/ These fears, however, are part of the New England heritage—the worst part—which leads the New Englander to become the Old Englander. Eliot's early life and work follow an almost hypnotic pattern; one might call him that pseudo-American, the type which finally won New England from the immigrant and gave it back to "history." The cultural dryness of New England was a by-product of this attitude which Eliot exemplifies even better than Henry James: that of relating America to New England, New England to England. Eliot was simply retracing the path back to Europe, exactly as Pound did, and as so many of our nineteenth-century writers tended to do, all but those specifically American.

The criticism of Eliot and Pound has blighted enormous literary areas, as far as we can tell.

The critics who helped establish Eliot were no less instrumental than Eliot himself in opening the frontiers of the cultural territory. Eliot with his palaver about the Tradition could gather in the entire Indo-European world, leaving North Asia and Africa to his senior. I do not want to go into the story of Eliot's critical rise to fame, but to illustrate what I mean I want to point to two literary critics who from every indication should have become his strongest foes; instead of becoming foes they were easily engaged to take his part in the high venture of Modern Poetic Culture. They are Edmund Wilson and F. O. Matthiessen.

Edmund Wilson may be fairly described as a critic in every way the natural opposite of Eliot. In his early estimate of Eliot in *Axel's Castle*, probably the first work to install Eliot in a high position in the literary mind, he pointed out almost every serious defect of the poet: his "fear of vulgarity," his intention to "depersonalize" literature, his overintellectu- /39/ ality, his obsessive imitativeness, and so forth. Wilson described Eliot as the Puritan-turned-artist and expressed the fear that the extravagant praise of Eliot on all sides would perhaps unbalance literary judgment, as of course it did. What then attracted Wilson to Eliot? *It was Eliot's influence on literary criticism.* Wilson walked straight into the trap which Eliot had baited for all humanists and run-of-the-mill men of letters. Eliot had written so high-mindedly about the literary past and so dolefully about the present that Wilson was taken in. He even began to praise Eliot's prose style—probably the worst prose style in the history of the English essay, as well as the most personal. What attracted the budding critic Wilson was, of course, the keenness of intelligence, the range of ideas, the feel of authority, and the sense of History. Also, a hopeful critic like Wilson was on the search for a poet to praise, and Wilson thought he had found him. Meanwhile Wilson was popped into the Eliot oven to be turned into a nice little, right little gingerbread man. Fortunately, he escaped, but that chapter does not belong to our chronicle.

F. O. Matthiessen's relationship to Eliot is even more extraordinary than that of the humanist critic who gazes in fascination at the Puritan-turned-artist. Matthiessen, I think, felt the same attraction for New England that Eliot did, the one coming from the West Coast, the other from the Midwest. To the critical and historical mind of Matthiessen, Eliot must have seemed an incarnation of American history. But Matthiessen had some adjusting to do in his own thinking in order to place Eliot in the same high position that Wilson had. He acknowledged his indebtedness to Wilson and also to I. A. Richards, the man who tried, and almost succeeded, in driving the poetic mind into the test tube. Matthiessen could not /40/ agree with Eliot's philosophy, his religion, or his politics, and yet he felt he must adulate Eliot! The result was his book on Eliot in which Matthiessen disdains the kind of criticism that deals with the poet's "ideas" and praises the kind of criticism that deals with the "forms." This book, *The Achievement of T. S. Eliot*, was published during the height of the Depression and at a time when Marxism was strong in the United States. Matthiessen was perhaps the most intensely engaged political mind among the English professors of his day, and a leftist; *yet he chose to cut himself off from the politics of Eliot's poetry and criticism to talk about the "forms."* This was a split that Eliot had invented for himself and which Eliot evidently kept from being fatal in his own life by various makeshifts of criticism. The false dualisms set up by Eliot between art and social action are symptomatic of the insanity of much modern criticism. In any case, it was Eliot's attractive formulation of these dualisms that neutralized so many critics and led Criticism itself into a squirrel cage where it still performs so brilliantly for its own amusement. Even Eliot's most favorable critics have never been able to resolve his major contradictions, which are central and irreducible conflicts rising from a false view of art as a function of history and culture, and a twisted attitude toward human nature.

Eliot's criticism is not "one thing" and his poetry another. They are one and the same. Herein lies the only unity of his work and of his "sensibility." This unity has been achieved coldly and ruthlessly, on paper. It has only as much relation to life as books can have: experience in Eliot is always and necessarily literary experience. All other experience is vulgar, with the possible exception of the religious experience, which is Eliot's escape hatch. His poems /41/ are therefore illustrations of the various stages of his "position," just as Pound's poems are illustrations of Pound's politick. Pound is not interested in poetry as poetry but in demonstrating what poetry is for. Eliot is above pedagogy, being closer to philosophy than to history. But the unifying element in Eliot is theology: and it is not inaccurate to describe Eliot as a theologian gone astray. The difference between Eliot's respectability and Pound's notoriety lies here as well. The frequent violence of Eliot's feelings is over-looked because of the "religious" context. Both his verse and his prose are held together by the main strength of certain theological abstractions. Eliot shows a positive hatred for originality and in fact condemns it in every manifestation; originality is irresponsible freedom to him. It is for this reason that he consigns Blake to limbo while hanging on to Pascal for dear life. Blake, says Eliot, is home-made religion. Eliot stays within the shadow of his theological law, which shelters his politics, his religion, and his esthetics.

How then is one to deal with his poetry without bringing in such terms as "mythic form," the "objective correlative," the "auditory imagination," the "dissociation of sensibility," the "Tradition," and fifty or sixty other concepts which are supposed to explain his poetry to us? The answer is by dealing with the poetry as poetry, as if Eliot had never published a single line of critical theory or laid down a single law or set up a single guidepost to "correct" taste. Ignore the criticism, if possible. Eliot's criticism, like all literary criticism, has a place in the seminar room in the philosophy department; let's keep it there. How it ever got out is a biographical question which we will leave to anyone daring enough to violate Eliot's fiat against biography. I take it that Eliot is /42/ mainly responsible for the modern taboo against literary biography, one of his less publicized fields of propaganda.

In another section of these notes I have made a distinction be-tween criticism and judgment. The strategic purpose of Eliot's criticism was to prevent judgment; that is the purpose of the criticism which he gave birth to (called the New Criticism), to re-place judgment by theory. Eliot's own judgment is seldom shown, governed as it is by precept. His intellectualization of feeling and taste led him to such twisted judgments as the praise of Kipling and the execration of Whitman, the approval of Donne and the dis-paragement of Milton, and to pronouncements such as "the novel died" on such and such a date. One of Eliot's followers, taking a suggestion from the master, writes a long, seemingly "objective" account of the weaknesses of the poetry of D. H. Lawrence. Lawrence had committed the horrible sin of expressing his own feelings in poetry. Instead of following "the discipline of a rationally constructed imagination," Lawrence *expresses*. If only, this critic complains, Lawrence had learned to use "controlled hysteria" like Eliot. And so forth. ("Controlled hysteria" strikes me as an accurate description of Eliot's poetry from an amateur psychology point of view, but the critic in question, R. P. Blackmur, egregiously takes Eliot's tightly buttoned-up pathology to be the normal state of affairs for poetry.)

To Eliot and Pound, with their provincial and educated horror of the unlettered and the spontaneous, the idea of a large or mixed audience was unspeakable. Throughout the criticism of these two leaders of modern taste the audience is constantly defined as a danger to the *status quo*. Pound, for example, in making up his booklist for converts to his criticism is /43/ even suspicious of the ballad. He cannot explain to himself that the ballad may be and probably is the product of the "unliterary" mind; he distrusts Shakespeare for the same reason. Eliot's own plays, of course, are addressed to a good sound upper-middle-class audience, British preferably, even though a couple of his dramatic works have a popular appeal. Eliot must get quite a chuckle out of that.

In discussing Eliot's or Pound's idea of the audience (or what they would call the *function* of literature, in their strangely mechanistic language) one runs into the old danger of bogging down in points of doctrine and definition. It is no exaggeration to say that Eliot's criticism contains a definite plan of action, leading from a theory of poetics to political philosophy and covering all the intermediate stages. I will come back to this matter in my remarks on Yeats and Pound and their part in the religion of modern poetry. As far as the audience is concerned it is enough to say Eliot and Pound have not really had one—Eliot not until a few years ago, Pound never. The public has consistently rejected all of the poetry of 1915-25 from the beginning and has ignored both the poetry and its scales of values. In the voluntary withdrawal of the audience, the critics have created an academic audience, that is, a captive audience. The true audience, when it is allowed to grow, may of course reach all levels of appreciation from the lowest to the highest; it is ever the job of the poet to address himself to the present *condition* of the audience and to the language of that audience. Eliot and Pound have both attempted to find the language of their time: both have failed miserably and have succeeded only in constructing parodistic copies of the language. (This is the cogent argument of William Carlos Williams against both poets.) /44/ Eliot's style of deliberate plagiarism is the first symptom of failure to locate the language—in his case a lifelong admission of defeat. Modern poetry is macaronic because, in fact, it is not linguistically modern at all. It is high time we related the Pound-Eliot antiquarianism in ideas to the antiquarianism of their styles. Pound uses more archaisms than the Poet Laureate of Florida.

I am going to deal with only a sample of the most typical and celebrated poems of Eliot's, from "Prufrock" through the *Quartets,* trying to *judge* these poems as if Eliot had never written any criticism. I judge them from the point of view of writing, on the assumption, which is to me a certainty, that all English-speaking people can appraise their worth as English poetry. This is the way poetry has always been read—without criticism or in spite of it. I disregard, as far as possible, Eliot's talk about the form of this and the form of that. I am confident that my judgments of these poems as poetry, not as sociology or esthetics, is extremely close to the judgments of nearly all readers of modern poetry who have not been conditioned by the criticism.

"The Love Song of J. Alfred Prufrock"—this is probably Eliot's best poem and is a little masterpiece of its kind. It is highly unoriginal in content and in style, based as it is on the rhythms, the attitudes, and sometimes the very lines of minor Symbolist poets like Corbière and Laforgue. Rhythmically it is the most successful of Eliot's poems, possibly because it was conceived as a dramatic unit. The meter is varied within the conventional English line, and the rhyming is superb. There is every indication that at the time of composition (age twenty-three) Eliot still took seriously the customs of English prosody and was trying in earnest (i.e., without irony) to develop this /45/ technical side of our poetry. The general tone of the poem is that of polite sophisticated ennui, an essay in self-mockery. The literary allusions in the poem, not counting the epigraph, are of the most obvious nature. This poem does not offend on the side of Culture. The epigraph from Dante purportedly throws a special light on the meaning of the poem; it is the epigraph which critics talk about most and which teachers teach. This quotation is gratuitous, a meaningless decoration; later it becomes the actual method of the Eliot poem. The difficulties of the poem, which are intentional, are not insurmountable, say, to a reader quite conversant with poetry tending toward the baroque or self-conscious. "Prufrock" is a poem *about* self-consciousness. The split personality of Prufrock creates the chief obstacle to a first understanding of the poem. The other primary difficulty is imagistic, but this is also the main virtue of the poem. The famous opening image of the evening prostrate "like a patient etherized upon a table" is one of the most brilliant examples of the poetry of exhaustion; very possibly it is a variation of Baudelaire's statement that the sexual act is like a surgical operation. Eliot's poem, however, is humorous rather than vicious and develops a kindly pathos to the very end. The imagery of the poem is all related to suggestion, a watering-down of the extreme suggestiveness of "effect" of poets like Mallarmé and Poe, and is, in fact, a retreat from official Symbolism. (Eliot would already be conscious of all the "historical" possibilities of his "position.") "Prufrock" is a masterpiece of a "period," the high point of Eliot's poetry. It is a true poem and also an experiment in criticism. It is a true poem by virtue of a personal content, which we can only guess at, for Eliot is always more sensitive about the autobiographical than any other writer /46/ I know of. But many things in the poem point to the so-called objectification of experience; even after Eliot airs to the public his problem of the personal and the impersonal, Life versus Art. The figure of Hamlet in "Prufrock" he finds particularly expressive of his own dilemma, even though Prufrock disclaims a true identity with the Prince. But Hamlet is the figure who makes an art of indecision. Indecision leads to thinking things over, soliloquizing, becoming an intellectual. Eliot's poetry all turns to talk. As it goes on through the years it becomes nothing but talk, and talk about the kind of poetry that comes closer and closer to talk. Technically, the poem prefigures all the criticism, with its debates about the personal and the impersonal, the more and more "objective," the great struggle toward "unified sensibility" and what not.

Eliot's failure as a poet is his success as a critic. Prufrock as a character is of no intrinsic interest but he is of high *literary* interest to all. In this poem Eliot has remained close enough to a human footing to make poetry out of a personal complex of crises, private, social, and intellectual. Had he written nothing else he would be remembered for this masterly little poem.

The "Portrait of a Lady" is also a young poem, written apparently at the time of "Prufrock." The "Portrait," however, is not a textbook piece; it is too much of a love poem. It is not as good a poem as "Prufrock," actually, because it has the tone of adolescence rather than the tone of a prefigured worldliness, as in "Prufrock." In the "Portrait" the woman is made fun of; she is wiser but inferior to the young Eliot; the poem leaves the reader nothing much to dwell upon except its excellence of execution. It appears to be one of Eliot's many exercises in tone. /47/ The epigraph in this case is a falsification. Eliot takes three lines from Marlowe's *The Jew of Malta,* the meaning of which he distorts for his own purpose. The lines are these:

> Thou hast committed—
> Fornication: but that was in another country,
> And besides, the wench is dead.

These three lines are actually part of a long involved dialogue; two people are speaking, not one. Eliot does not mean to convey that only one person is speaking, but he must for convenience gloze over the sense of the play. Eliot exegetes can retrace the quotation and explain that a friar is accusing the traitorous Jew, Barabas, of a series of crimes and that the Jew is evading answering; in the same way the Eliot in the poem is evading answering the questions of the woman. Psychologically this kind of thing can become so involved that everything reverts back to the meaning of the quotation. This is the crux of the Eliot poem, as we all know: how does the quotation fit the poem? Very shortly the matter is reversed and the question becomes: how does the poem fit the *quotation?* The beauty of the "Portrait" testifies to Eliot's residual interest in the poem, not in its possible intellectual overtones; the quotation (virtually a misquotation) also indicates the poet's concern about what he writes rather than what he quotes. But the quote is also a loophole for the meaning of the poem, permitting Eliot to evade his meaning or permitting critics to elaborate it.

In both of these poems Eliot displays a mastery of sound and rhythm which marks the poet of genius. The rhyming is dazzling, a mixture of shock (the use of near-comic pairs such as Pole-soul) and the much more subtle effect of nonrhyme, such as we find in /48/ "Lycidas." It is almost, but not quite, apparent that Eliot at the beginning of his career is playing the weary virtuoso. But this is not sufficient, either for Eliot or for the literary scene. There is not much to be gained by becoming another Anglo-American Laforgue.

The remaining poems of this early style are even more "French" than the longer ones, but more satisfying evidently to Eliot. "Preludes" introduces the typical sordid furniture of the Eliot world, a Baudelairean rather than Laforguean world. The poem is a series of images evoking despair and disgust. The popularity of the poem comes from its seriousness, the transference from youthful, well-educated ennui to a genuine, if not very thoughtful, revulsion for all those people "raising dingy shades in a thousand furnished rooms." Eliot here imports the clichés of nineteenth-century French poetry about the wickedness (i.e., mediocrity) of the modern city. "Rhapsody on a Windy Night," a much more convincing poem, dramatizes and symbolizes the horror of the city. Eliot has already found the Culture of the modern city; by simply recording its images (a broken spring in a factory yard, a morsel of rancid butter, the toothbrush hanging on the wall) he evokes a cultured response—the response of the *avant-garde* reader to society. It is assumed, without having to say so, that the modern city is a degeneration of the Past. *Now he knows what to say:* the housemaids have "damp" souls; people await the evening paper for want of something better, the old order changeth and Cousin Nancy has taken to smoking; the poet is quietly rejecting both the present and the immediate past— the American past.

The first really literary poem comes in this phase also. (I use the term "literary" opprobriously.) "Mr. /49/ Apollinax" marks the new Eliot; the Greek epigraph becomes an integral part of the poem, an explanation of it; and there is no attempt to provide links from the reader's experience to the cultural cues. The meter begins to break and the rhymes are now artfully coarsened (afternoon-macaroon). Mr. Apollinax is something of a pagan oracle to Eliot and a Priapic figure, but not to the Boston professors who entertain him. The poem is inferior to the "Rhapsody" in every way; it is already a culture poem and an exercise in footnoting.

Eliot's reputation to a large extent is based upon the poems of this early period, and rightly so. "Prufrock," "Portrait of a Lady," "Preludes," and the "Rhapsody" are among his best works. Of these "Prufrock" is head and shoulders above the rest and is sufficient to justify Eliot's claim as one of the most gifted twentieth-century poets. At the same time it is extremely close to *vers de société,* as the first reviewers were aware (and first impressions are generally valuable in literary criticism), while the other poems mentioned are almost mannerist in their attention to theory and precedent. These are true weaknesses and Eliot is evidently conscious of their defects, the proof being that he deserts these forms for new ones.

In the next phase we find the majority of the poems in pedantic and ironic quatrains. There is one attempt at a "major" form, as the critics say, in the poem "Gerontion," and there are several poems in French, which certainly cannot be judged as English poems. The quatrain poems introduce Sweeney and various minor characters in Eliot's pantheon. In this group there is also the extraordinarily crude anti-church poem named "The Hippopotamus," one of those

surprising lapses of Eliot's which almost equal /50/ his good poems
in number. Equally crude is the embarrassing anti-Jewish poem
"Burbank with a Baedeker," a typical utterance of the modern
"classical" school. Eliot's anti-Semitism, which I am not going to
discuss, is connected with his view of American commercial wealth:
Bleistein is "Chicago Semite Viennese" and he is described in dis-
gusting physical detail. It is interesting to note that as Eliot's
feelings become more violent and shocking the epigraphic matter
becomes more talky and deranged. The quotation affixed to this
poem is a hodgepodge of a French poem, a Latin motto, something
from Henry James, something from Shakespeare, something from
Browning, and something from Marston. It is as obscure as the
quatrains are clear. The Chicago Shylock and the British baronet
with a Jewish name have taken back Venice, according to this
culture lyric. Stylistically and otherwise there is little virtue in the
piece.

Stylistically there is little or nothing of value in all the quatrain
poems, "Sweeney Erect," "A Cooking Egg," "Whispers of Immor-
tality," "Mr. Eliot's Sunday Morning Service," and the famous
"Sweeney Among the Nightingales." In these poems Eliot is exploring the possibilities of character symbols; most turn out to be
mere caricatures and do not appear again. Sweeney survives as a
representation of Eliot's dim view of modern man. Eliot tries humor
in the poems, if humor is the proper word (a highly polysyllabic
bumbling kind of pseudo-British joking); and this he alternates
with scenes of horror and disorder made ironical by the propriety
of the meters. The close of the "Nightingale" poem is said by
critics to mark a high point of nobility, why I am not sure, unless it
is that Eliot leaves off "Rachel *née* Rabinovitch" and switches to
Agamemnon and the Convent of the Sacred Heart. These closing
lines, if indeed /51/ they are serious, are cheap rather than noble and
so poorly articulated that they can barely be pronounced. These
poems show a drastic falling-off from the poet's earlier work. (I
have said nothing of the complexities of cultural allusion in these
poems; most people know them and accept them as part of the rocky
road to modern poetry.)

"Gerontion" is usually placed high among Eliot's works; but it
is not much better than "Mr. Apollinax" and is in fact an extension
of that poem in its manner. In order to escape a derivative Symbolism, Eliot has settled on the borrowing of quotations. Without a
knowledge of the sources the poems sound more or less unified; the
quotations themselves remove some of the author's responsibility

for what the poems say. Eliot was here working out a method for a kind of poem which would implant certain ideas and images in the reader's mind, almost as if Eliot himself had nothing to do with the poem. The use of quotation without reference has a further advantage: it creates a specialized class of readers; I am quite serious when I say that Eliot is here providing texts for a new academic faculty. In the same way as Pound he is trying to solve an educational problem. But "Gerontion" is also a personal catechism of the poet's religious hopes and doubts and is part of his spiritual autobiography. Its best feature is the rhetorical accretion of the same grammatical form and the use of meaningless but suggestive names. The theme of the youthless-ageless man, which is Eliot's one contribution to symbology, is advanced again, as in all his earlier poems. There is in "Gerontion" a careful propaganda for Eliot as a symbolic figure, the poet deep in thought, seated among the ruins of the ages, longing for a salvation which will suit his intellect as well as his desires for spiritual comfort. /52/

The Waste Land is the most important poem of the twentieth century, that is, the one that has caused the most discussion and is said by critics to be the culmination of the modern "mythic" style. The poem, by Eliot's own admission, is a collaboration with Pound. Pound edited it and removed a third or two thirds of it. The "continuity," we can assume, is therefore the work of Pound, who abhorred continuity in his own more ambitious poetry. As everyone knows how to read the poem or can find out by visiting the nearest library, I will say nothing about its meaning. I will speak rather of the success and the failure of the poem. That it is lacking in unity is obvious (assuming, as I do, that unity is a literary virtue). Any part of The Waste Land can be switched with any other part without changing the sense of the poem. Aside from the so-called "mythic" form, which is worthless and not even true—for Eliot misread James Joyce's Ulysses when he saw it as a parallel to Homer—the underlying unit of the poem is tonal and dramatic, exactly as a Victorian narrative poem would be. Eliot tries to conceal this indispensable literary method by mixing languages, breaking off dramatic passages, and by dividing the poem into sections with titles. But what really keeps the poem moving is its rhetoric, its switches from description to exclamation to interrogation to expletive, sometimes very beautifully, as in the passages beginning "Unreal City." The straight descriptive passages are weak: "A Game of Chess" is one of the dullest and most meretricious of Eliot's writings, indicating his own dissatisfaction with that kind of verse. The dialogue, on the other hand, is generally good. The best moments of all are the image passages, where the images are set in dramatic tonalities: "What the Thunder Said" is the finest of these. The very worst passages /53/ are those which are merely quotes; even Eliot's most abject admirers can find no justification of the last lines of the poem, with its half-dozen languages and more than half a dozen quotations in a space of about ten lines.

The Waste Land, because of its great critical reputation, not because of any inherent worth it might have, is one of the curiosities of English literature. Its critical success was, I dare say, carefully planned and executed, and it was not beyond the realm of possibility that the poem was originally a hoax, as some of the first readers insisted. But hoax or not, it was very shortly made the sacred cow of modern poetry and the object of more pious literary nonsense than any modern work save the Cantos of Pound. The proof of the failure of the "form" of this poem is that no one has ever been able to proceed from it, including Eliot himself. It is, in fact, not a form at all but a negative version of form. It is interesting to notice that in the conventional stanzas of the quatrain poems Eliot is more personally violent and ugly about his own beliefs; in his unconventional style the voice of the poet all but disappears and is replaced by characters from his reading.

The emergence of Eliot's piety in "The Hollow Men" and in Ash Wednesday takes the form of self-disgust in the one and self-pity in the other. "The Hollow Men" is in every way a better poem than The Waste Land, though the parodistic style again enforces a poverty of statement and language which become the marks of self-imitation in Eliot. Ash Wednesday is probably even more laden with gratuitous quotation than The Waste Land, but its ecclesiastical imagery and richness of music give the poem a beauty which the poet can finally accept as beauty. Eliot here luxuriates in the emotions of piety and sur- /54/ render which seemed shameful to his Puritan soul in a purely human situation. The Eliot-God equation, once he has made the daring step, gives him an intellectual-emotional balance for the first time in his career. After the publication of this poem, Eliot's former work seems more of a piece and his future work is all laid out for him, everything from church pageants to Christmas-card poems. The Ariel Poems are relatively simple and almost narrative. The rest of the poems are shelved under "fragments," minor pieces, and unfinished experiments. Eliot's career as a poet virtually comes to a close with Ash Wednesday. After that there is criticism, theology, and drama. The Four

Quartets is the only attempt at what modern criticism calls a "major" poem—meaning a poem that deals with Culture wholesale. The *Quartets* were hailed by the Eliot critics as his crowning achievement; actually they are evidence of the total dissolution of poetic skill and even a confession of poetic bankruptcy. Eliot is quite open about this in the *Quartets*.

The *Quartets* are Eliot's bid to fame as a "philosophical poet." In it he expounds his metaphysics, his poetics, and his own place in the scheme of things. All of this is quite legitimate and not at all surprising; what is disturbing about the poems is their common-placeness, their drabness of expression, their conventionality, and, worst of all, their reliance on the schoolbook language of the philosophy class. Eliot has traded poetry for the metaphysical abstraction, as in *The Waste Land* he had traded narrative for "myth." This development is psychologically consistent, a descent from French Symbolism to Metaphysical complexity-for-the-sake-of-complexity, to pastiche, to the myth-science of *The Golden Bough,* to philosophical abstraction without poetic content. It all /55/ ends in the complete abandonment of poetry. When he comes to the drama in earnest he knows, of course, that he must use human language and he begins a new ascent into literature and the voices of poetry. But the *Quartets* lie at the bottom of the literary heap. All the so-called lyric sections, with one or two exceptions, are written with such disregard for the ear that one cannot associate them with the Eliot of "Prufrock" or the "Rhapsody." "Garlic and sapphires in the mud/ Clot the bedded axle-tree" is typical of this diction devoid of both image and music. Eliot, who used to condemn poets like Tennyson for what he called crudeness of feeling, here shows an insensitivity toward language which is marvelous. The more prosy passages are even voided of that kind of poetry which rises from the use of imagery or sound. As for the philosophical development, it fails to reach a state of poetry, and it may fail as philosophy—of this I am no judge. The much-quoted third section of "East Coker" about everyone going into the darkness, even people in the Almanach de Gotha and the Stock Exchange Gazette, is possibly the best passage of a long, very bad piece of writing; one feels that here there is an acceptance of the badness of the writing, as if good writing no longer held any meaning for the poet. The "lyric" section that follows contains a stanza ("The whole earth is our hospital/Endowed by the ruined millionaire . . .") which in its vulgarity of thought and expression is hardly superior to "Only God can make a tree." For the rest there is a kind of narcissistic figure of the aging Eliot lolling through the poem, the climactic Dante imitation in "Little Gidding," and finally the magnificent passage "Sin is Behovely, but/ All shall be well . . ." Unfortunately these glorious lines are not Eliot's but are one of his borrowings. In general, the *Four Quartets* ap- /56/ pears to be a deliberately bad book, one written as if to convince the reader that poetry is dead and done with. We should remember Eliot's lifelong interest in the final this and the final that, and at least entertain the possibility that the *Four Quartets* were intended to stand as the last poem in the Great Tradition. Eliot and Pound have both shown themselves capable of such arrogance.

I have now said all the wicked things I can think of about Eliot and it remains at last to say something favorable. At the beginning of these remarks I mentioned one phase of Eliot's work in which I regard him as a true poet and a man of rich spiritual insight. While I cannot feel that Eliot has contributed anything to the spiritual advancement of our age, I am convinced that he tried. But why is it that his own poems are rubrics rather than works of art? What are they for? What are they trying to say? Is it really all just sociology, reactionary politics, bitterness, spite and despair? I think not. I have spoken of the apparently deliberate erosion of his great gifts, leading to the final desertion of poetry. And I have touched on Eliot's lapse into religion. Here is a capital puzzle for the critic.

My solution to the puzzle is this. The motivating force in Eliot's work is the search for the mystical center of experience. This search in his case has been fruitless and increasingly frustrating. Eliot's entire career is a history of his failure to penetrate the mystical consciousness. He begins as a youth with Symbolism when it is already a dying religious-esthetic *mystique*. He moves from Symbolism to the Metaphysical poets of the seventeenth century. (Neither the dictionary nor modern criticism explains what it is that interested Eliot in these poets, for it certainly /57/ was not extreme metaphorical technique or what the textbook calls the conceit.) Eliot was fascinated by the Metaphysical poem because it is virtually a demonstration of prayer. Nearly all the Metaphysical poets were Divines, men deeply troubled by the new scientific knowledge. What Eliot studied in their poetry was the possibility of fusing sacred with secular knowledge in poetry. Metaphysical poetry lies close to absurdity because it is premised on this peculiar dualism. We recall also that Eliot associated the fairly recent French poet Laforgue with the English Metaphysicals, for at one time it seemed to Eliot that a keen enough wit might serve as a key to the door that refused to open. But neither Symbolism nor Metaphysical sacred poetry offered a way to Eliot, even when he tried a fusion of the two. Third, he attempted secular mythology as a way to penetrate the mystical consciousness. It was in this phase that he wrote *The Waste Land,* a poem which is a jumble of sacred and "profane" myths, adding up to nothing.

Meanwhile, both Eliot and Pound had discovered T. E. Hulme, whose essays provided written authority for them both, in different ways. Every major doctrine of Eliot's can be found in Hulme's *Speculations,* the most basic the one that relates fundamental Christian doctrine to a theory of society and a theory of poetics. Hulme formulated for Eliot the attack on Romanticism and the attack on mysticism (for the Romantic and the mystical are always related, while the Classical and the orthodox are related in their ways, at least in the critical mind). Hulme pointed the way for Eliot to orthodoxy in letters and to ritual and dogma in the spiritual realm. I consider Hulme's book as the *Mein Kampf* of modern criticism and a thoroughly evil work; and it was Eliot's undoing. For after the assimi- /58/ lation of Hulme, the rest is elaboration. Except for one thing: the search for the mystical center of experience goes on. Eliot worries it in Dante, in the Hindu scriptures, in St. John of the Cross, and in Julianne of Norwich. But poets of more recent vintage who come closer to mysticism infuriate Eliot, and he pours out his scorn on Blake, Lawrence, Whitman and our own Transcendentalists. Yet it is eternally to Eliot's credit that he does not fake the mystical (as he seems to accuse Blake of doing) and it is also to his credit that he does not relapse into magic and spiritualism, as Yeats did. It appears that Eliot is not even acquainted with esotericism; at least he does not even seem to be conscious of the esoteric meaning of the Tarot, which he uses in *The Waste Land* for "fortunetelling."

The failure to achieve mystical consciousness (which indeed is one of the rarest achievements in mankind) drove Eliot back to metaphysics proper and to religion proper. This in my view is the great failure of Eliot. Eliot ends up as a poet of religion in the conventional sense of that term. And once having made the religious commitment he tried to visualize a religion-directed society; he thus becomes an official of the most conservative elements of society and a figurehead for all that is formalized and ritualized. Yeat's fascination for the Byzantine betrays the same spiritual conservatism, as does Pound's fascination for the corporate state and the leadership principle. And Eliot ends his quest with his caricature of the modern poet-priest or psychiatrist-priest who alone has power to allay the

Eumenides. Witch-hunting runs through Eliot from beginning to end.

Eliot is a poet of religion, hence a poet of the second or third rank; he is a thoroughgoing anachronism in the modern world, a poet of genius crippled /59/ by lack of faith and want of joy. I believe in Blake's proverb that "the road of excess leads to the palace of wisdom." Had Eliot ever set foot on that road he might have been as great a seer as Whitman or Rimbaud or even Dylan Thomas. /60/

QUESTIONS FOR READING AND WRITING

Kenner: How the Poem Was Constructed

1. Contrast the political-economic state of Europe in 1921 with its cultural state. Who were some of the writers, painters, and musicians then flourishing? See Hough's essay for some literary figures.
2. What did Pound mean by calling *The Waste Land* "the longest poem in the English langwidge"?
3. If it is true that the poet finds unity in seeming diversity, can *The Waste Land* be attributed as much to Pound as to Eliot? Why not?

Maxwell: How the Poem Was Received and Its Critical Issues Defined

1. Is it possible to "look directly on life" without the "spectacles of books" or other instruction? In what sense does a poem, a painting, a story shape our awareness of the world?
2. Explain how literature "transcends our experience."
3. Define *theosophy;* refer to dictionaries and other works of general reference.
4. How does this — or any poem for that matter — place "aspects of civilisation . . . in the perspective of time"?

Wasserstrom: How the Poem Appeared in America

1. Wasserstrom distinguishes two schools of letters: Pound, Ransom, and Tate as opposed to Van Wyck Brooks and William Carlos Williams. What is the issue separating them?
2. What was it in Eliot's writing that attracted Thayer? How did *The Waste Land* suit his purposes?
3. Does the information in this essay confirm Shapiro's contention that Eliot's reputation rests on conspiracy, at least in part?

Leavis: The Poem's Unity

1. Explain what Leavis means by the "remoteness of the civilization celebrated in *The Waste Land* from the natural rhythms." Explain the meaning of this statement: "To be, then, too much conscious and conscious of too much — that is the plight."

2. According to Leavis, for what purposes are the Tarot cards introduced? Does his explanation square with Kenner's comments on the notes to the poem?
3. In what sense is this poem filled with a "hallucinatory quality"?
4. Explain: "The unity the poem aims at is that of an inclusive consciousness."
5. Is Leavis distressed that the poem is not "available" to readers generally? How does one come to a "full response" to it?
6. Explain Eliot's remark, as quoted in the footnote, that "genuine poetry can communicate before it is understood."
7. Does Leavis see the poem as offering any promise of redemption? According to him, what is the nature of the age "out of which the poem grew"?

Matthiessen: The System of Allusion

1. Explain the meaning and relevance of the epigraph.
2. In what sense can one be "too frightened to be honest"?
3. How can a knowledge of the past lead to chaos? To a "sense of the potential unity of life"?
4. What did Eliot learn from anthropology, according to Matthiessen? How does this knowledge help in "compressing"? Compressing *what*?
5. According to Matthiessen and Eliot, how does poetry differ from prose?
6. Explain what Matthiessen means by saying that: "the mature artist finds his strength partly by coming to recognize and reckon with his limitations." Is this peculiar to artists?
7. How does Matthiessen defend Eliot against charges that he does not appeal to a "popular audience"? That he lacks spontaneity? That he is bookish?
8. According to Matthiessen, how does one best begin to read Eliot?
9. In what sense are Eliot's notes to the poem superfluous and even misleading?
10. Explain: "Try to be one of the people on whom nothing is lost!"

Brooks: The Beliefs Embodied in the Work

1. Compare Brooks's analysis with Leavis's to discover what some of Leavis's "positive errors of interpretation" are. See especially the last few paragraphs of Brooks's essay.

2. Explain the difference between "rationalization" of form and the poem itself.
3. What is the central paradox of the poem as Brooks reads it? In what sense is spiritual death attractive?
4. Into how many parts does Brooks divide his analysis of Section I of the poem? In what central ways are the parts related to one another?
5. What is the relationship of the two major parts of Section II?
6. In what way is Ophelia like the woman in the pub, as Brooks asserts?
7. What is the central symbol of Section III? How is it related to the foregoing sections of the poem?
8. Explain: "Modern man, freed from all restraints, in his cultivation of experience for experience's sake burns, but not with a 'hard and gemlike flame.'"
9. List the symbolic contrasts between Section III and Section IV.
10. By what means is a sense of horror built up in Section V? How is the description of the waste land at the end of the poem different from its initial introduction, according to Brooks?
11. Explain: "The basic method used in *The Waste Land* may be described as the application of the principle of complexity." How does "ambiguity" demonstrate the poet's "fidelity to the complexity of experience"?
12. Eliot, unlike Spenser, foregoes didacticism preferring "to stick to the poet's business." What is that?

Schwartz: T. S. Eliot as the International Hero

1. According to Schwartz's definition, are there other literary "culture heroes" in our time? Is Faulkner one? Hemingway?
2. In what way is "literary allusion . . . a powerful and inevitable habit of mind"?
3. "We have become an international people." Is this fundamentally true? Are American servicemen "at home" abroad? Are Europeans "at home" in America?
4. What are some of the major themes in Eliot's poetry? Are they the themes that Brooks identifies as central in *The Waste Land*?
5. Explain the relationship of deracination to the inability of the international man to love.
6. Explain the paradox in the statement: "We are all the bankrupt heirs of the ages."

Hough: Imagism and Its Consequences

1. What does Hough think is the relation of the creation of literature to society? Is it simple?
2. Is the "poetic conspiracy" of which Hough speaks the same kind of conspiracy to which Shapiro refers?
3. What is "literary tradition" according to Hough? Have the "men of 1914" established one?
4. What connection does Hough make between Symbolism and magic? Between Imagism and magic?
5. What did Eliot mean by the "objective correlative"? How is it related to Imagism?
6. In what way are the terms "logic of emotion" and "logic of imagination" a straining of *logic*?
7. Does Kenner or Brooks or another defender of the poem deny the "logical discontinuity" and the "rhetorical incongruities" of *The Waste Land*? Why does Hough disallow them? Explain the meaning of the phrase "the ordinary modes of rational communication."

Craig: The Defeatism of *The Waste Land*

1. In what sense is *The Waste Land* an invitation to snobbery? How does Matthiessen answer this argument?
2. Discuss the ways in which the irony of the poem is facile, according to Craig.
3. In what sense does Craig regard the Eliot of *The Waste Land* as a Puritan? Compare with Sir Toby Belch's criticism of Malvolio: "Dost thou think, because thou art virtuous, there shall be no more cakes and ale?" *(Twelfth Night,* II, iii, 123-125)
4. Explain: "It is primitivist; and it thoughtlessly ignores the experience involved."
5. "Therefore the only positive course is to co-operate with the hopeful present trends." What are some of the "present trends" to which Craig might be referring?
6. Schwartz and others to the contrary, Craig maintains that this poem "is *not* the representative work of the present age." How does he arrive at this conclusion? What works do you think he might regard as "representative"? Does he make any suggestions?

Shapiro: The Death of Literary Judgment

1. Explain: "In other words, Eliot invented a Modern World. . . .
   Insofar as Eliot has enjoyed a *poetic* influence, it lies outside
   literature entirely and is what can only be called a 'spiritual'
   influence." Is Shapiro agreeing with Schwartz that Eliot is a
   "culturel hero"?
2. According to Shapiro, why is "criticism of [Eliot's] poetry
   impossible"?
3. Explain: "For it is criticism which is the twentieth-century
   substitute for poetry." Do Shapiro and Brooks agree on the
   function of poetry?
4. Why may a horror of "the unlettered and the spontaneous" be
   said to be "provincial and educated"? What does the word
   "educated" mean here?
5. What is the relation of Eliot's language to current speech
   according to Shapiro? After referring to the poem, would you
   say his judgments are sound?
6. In what sense is Eliot's early work *vers de société*? Can *The
   Waste Land* be said to be of this type?
7. In what way is Shapiro's criticism of the unity of *The Waste
   Land* similar to Hough's?
8. In what way can it be said that a "parodistic style . . . enforces
   a poverty of statement and language"? What is "self-imitation"?
9. Explain: "The motivating force in Eliot's work is the search
   for the mystical center of experience." Can this be related to
   what Leavis identifies as the "hallucinatory quality" in the
   poem?

SELECTED BIBLIOGRAPHY

Bibliography

Gallup, Donald. *T. S. Eliot: A Bibliography.* New York: Harcourt, Brace & World, Inc., 1953. Indispensable.

Brief general accounts of poet and work

Bradbrook, M. C. *T. S. Eliot.* Rev. ed. (Writers and Their Work, No. 8.) London: Longmans, Green & Company for The British Council, 1955. Contains information and critical bibliographies.
Unger, Leonard. *T. S. Eliot.* (Pamphlets on American Writers, No. 8.) Minneapolis: University of Minnesota Press, 1961. Contains notable critical comments and brief bibliographies.

Collections of general critical essays

Kenner, Hugh, ed. *T. S. Eliot: A Collection of Critical Essays.* (Twentieth Century Views.) Englewood Cliffs, N.J.: Prentice-Hall, Inc., 1962. Nineteen essays, most of which are by fervent admirers of the work.
Unger, Leonard, ed. *T. S. Eliot: A Selected Critique.* New York: Holt, Rinehart & Winston, Inc., 1948. Thirty-one selections by critics and critic-professors. Considers most of important work to the date of Nobel Prize and includes bibliographies of secondary work to date of publication.

Discussions of *The Waste Land*

Alvarez, Alfred. *Stewards of Excellence: Studies in Modern English and American Poets.* New York: Charles Scribner's Sons, 1958, pp. 11-32. Also published as *The Shaping Spirit,* London, Chatto & Windus, 1958. The relation of the poem to "tradition."
Beringause, A. F. "Journey Through *The Waste Land,*" *South Atlantic Quarterly,* Vol. 56 (1957), pp. 79-90. The immediate Victorian antecedents of the poem.
Bowra, C. M. *The Creative Experiment.* London: The Macmillan Company, 1949, pp. 159-188.
Brown, Alec. "The Lyric Impulse in the Poetry of T. S. Eliot," *Scrutinies,* Vol. 2. (1931), pp. 34-48.

Collingwood, R. G. *The Principles of Art.* Oxford: Clarendon Press, 1938, pp. 331-336. The poem as illustrative of esthetic theories.

Deutsch, Babette. *Poetry in Our Time.* 2nd ed., rev. and enl. Garden City, N.Y.: Doubleday & Company, Inc., 1963, pp. 173-178.

Drew, Elizabeth. *T. S. Eliot: The Design of His Poetry.* New York: Charles Scribner's Sons, 1949, pp. 58-90. A Jungian interpretation.

Friar, Kimon, and John Malcolm Brinnin. *Modern Poetry: American and British.* New York: Appleton-Century-Crofts, Inc., 1951, pp. 425-426, 472-497. An analytic paraphrase for beginning readers.

Hoffman, Frederick J. *The Twenties: American Writing in the Postwar Decade.* New York: The Viking Press, 1955, pp. 291-303. The poem as exemplifying doubt in the Twenties.

Kenner, Hugh. *The Invisible Poet: T. S. Eliot.* New York: Ivan Obolensky, Inc., 1959, pp. 152-182.

Lucy, Sean. *T. S. Eliot and the Idea of Tradition.* New York: Barnes & Noble, Inc., 1960, pp. 153-159. Concentrates on echoes and influences.

MacCallum, H. Reid. "The Waste Land after Twenty-five Years," *Here and Now,* Vol. 1 (1947), pp. 16-24. A "defense" by interpretation of details and meaning.

Maxwell, D. E. S. *The Poetry of T. S. Eliot.* New York: Barnes & Noble, Inc., 1961, pp. 100-117. Concentrates on the symbolism of the poem.

Moorman, Charles. *Arthurian Triptych: Mythic Materials in Charles Williams, C. S. Lewis, and T. S. Eliot.* (Perspectives in Criticism 5.) Berkeley and Los Angeles: University of California Press, 1960, pp. 127-148. The poem as "a sacramental fusing of image and idea."

Moynihan, William T., "The Goal of the Waste Land Quest," *Renascence,* Vol. 13 (1961), pp. 171-179. Concentrates on the epic and mystical levels of the quest.

Nelson, A. H. "The Critics and *The Waste Land,* 1922-1949," *English Studies,* Vol. 36 (1955), pp. 1-15. A bibliographical essay which summarizes and classifies.

Smidt, Kristian. *Poetry and Belief in the Work of T. S. Eliot.* Oslo: Jacob Dybwad, 1949, pp. 121-125. The poem as an expression of a recurring psychic state.

Smith, Grover C. *T. S. Eliot's Poetry and Plays.* Chicago: University of Chicago Press, 1956, pp. 67-98. Concentrates on sources.

Thomas, Wright, and Stuart Gerry Brown. *Reading Poems: An Introduction to Critical Study.* New York: Oxford University Press, 1941, pp. 716-731, 749-751. An analytic paraphrase for beginning students.

Traversi, Derek. *"The Waste Land* Revisited: A Critical Analysis of Mr. Eliot's Work," *Dublin Review,* No. 443 (1948), pp. 106-123. The poem seen in relation to Eliot's subsequent work.

Williamson, George. *A Reader's Guide to T. S. Eliot.* New York: The Noonday Press, 1953, pp. 115-154. A careful passage-by-passage interpretation minimizing anthropological framework.

Wilson, Edmund. *Axel's Castle.* New York: Charles Scribner's Sons, 1931, pp. 104-111. The first general critical estimation.

Wilson, Frank. *Six Essays on the Development of T. S. Eliot.* London: The Fortune Press, 1948, pp. 23-41. The musical structure of the poem.

Winters, Yvor. *The Anatomy of Nonsense.* Norfolk, Conn.: New Directions, 1943, pp. 162-167. A wholesale attack on both form and content of the poem.

Wright, George. *The Poet in the Poem.* (Perspectives in Criticism 4.) Berkeley and Los Angeles: University of California Press, 1960, pp. 60-76. The characteristics and function of the *personae* in the poem.